HIS MOTHER TRAINED HIM TO KILL
JESUS TOUGHT HIM TO LOVE

BAD TO THE BONE
ENRAPTURED
by
LOVE

The True Story of Rev. George Freeman

THE POWER OF REDEMPTION

GEORGE FREEMAN

WestBow
Press®
A DIVISION OF THOMAS NELSON
& ZONDERVAN

Copyright © 2019 George Freeman.

All rights reserved. No part of this book may be used or reproduced by any means, graphic, electronic, or mechanical, including photocopying, recording, taping or by any information storage retrieval system without the written permission of the author except in the case of brief quotations embodied in critical articles and reviews.

This book is a work of non-fiction. Unless otherwise noted, the author and the publisher make no explicit guarantees as to the accuracy of the information contained in this book and in some cases, names of people and places have been altered to protect their privacy.

WestBow Press books may be ordered through booksellers or by contacting:

WestBow Press
A Division of Thomas Nelson & Zondervan
1663 Liberty Drive
Bloomington, IN 47403
www.westbowpress.com
1 (866) 928-1240

Because of the dynamic nature of the Internet, any web addresses or links contained in this book may have changed since publication and may no longer be valid. The views expressed in this work are solely those of the author and do not necessarily reflect the views of the publisher, and the publisher hereby disclaims any responsibility for them.

Any people depicted in stock imagery provided by Getty Images are models, and such images are being used for illustrative purposes only. Certain stock imagery © Getty Images.

The Authorized (King James) Version of the Bible ('the KJV'), the rights in which are vested in the Crown in the United Kingdom, is reproduced here by permission of the Crown's patentee, Cambridge University Press.

ISBN: 978-1-9736-7530-3 (sc)
ISBN: 978-1-9736-7529-7 (hc)
ISBN: 978-1-9736-7531-0 (e)

Print information available on the last page.

WestBow Press rev. date: 10/08/2019

DEDICATION

ALL THAT IS NECESSARY FOR EVIL TO TRIUMPH IS FOR GOOD MEN TO DO NOTHING

THIS BOOK IS DEDICATED TO THOSE IN MY LIFE WHO INSPIRED ME TO STAND ON THE ROCK, TO REACH FOR THE TOP. TO GET OUT OF THE HORRIBLE PIT I HAD GOTTEN MYSELF INTO THROUGH HATE, AND UNFORGIVENESS.

Brenton Burgoyne Freeman

The greatest father any boy could know

The Resident State Trooper Ludwig Kolodziej.1958.

My first Pastor DePot Baptist Church

Pastor David Ferrero, Mansfield DePot

The teachers of ZION Bible Institute

The prophet Bill Britain, Springfield, Mo.

Pastor Richard Wilson, West Virginia

With special thanks to Darren Abraham, Dick Ritter, Robert Phillips; and the staff at WestBow Press for their help in the publication of this book.

With much love and appreciation to my family; My wife Sandra Freeman, Nathan, his wife Stacie, Samuel, his wife Cheryl, Seth, Caleb, Courtney, and Josh. For all the love, care, help and support you have given me over the years. Thank you from the bottom of my heart.

Then said Jesus to Thomas "Reach hither thy finger, and behold my hands; and reach hither thy hand, and thrust it into my side; and be not faithless but believing."

Zechariah 13:6. "And one shall say unto him, What are these wounds in thine hands? Then he shall answer those with which I was wounded in the house of my friends."

WOUNDED IN THE HOUSE OF MY FRIENDS

Hello, my name is George Freeman. The story you are about to read is true. It is life as I experienced it. I have changed many of the names to protect the innocent, as well as the guilty. There are parts that I have softened for the readers' sake, but it still has some very bad twists and turns.

I felt it necessary to include some explicit subjects in a delicate manner, because we are living in a world that has gone bad, very bad.

We have a society that chooses to cloak the evil of child abuse, under the guise of diversity's, of lifestyle. The hard, fact is that parental and spouse abuse has given us, Prostitutes, By-polar, Serial rapists, Serial killers, alcoholics, drug addicts, the whole LGBTQ-XYZ group including violent people that believe that bullying is the way of life. No one is born emotionally deficient in these areas.

ALL BEHAVIOR IS LEARNED BEHAVIOR

Some of you will say that I am wrong for lumping this group of people into one group. You will correctly say that some of these are criminals that some are mentally challenged, that some are just of a different life style; and that is all true. But the reason that I have put them all into one group is that they all have one thing in common. In order for them to live as they do; they were all abused or neglected by their parents or guardians. They are outside the realm of what Doctors call normal, because of abuse, or abandonment as because of divorce or as the case of a parent on drugs. I know, firsthand, because my mother was training me to kill.

Jesus Christ gave me a second chance. He also gave to me the privilege of watching Him do some pretty awesome things to just ordinary people, like yourself. He saved, healed, cast out demons, yes even raised the dead, and He did it all because He loves us. We are all in trouble and Jesus died to rescue us all.

I won't blame you if you read this book through the eyes of a sceptic. I would have too before I met Jesus for myself. When I was baptized with the Holy Spirit, I had no past spiritual experience. I came to realize that Satan will not build up the Kingdom of God, neither will Jesus tear down His own Kingdom. We have His word on that. We are living in the "New Testament age". From the moment that Jesus died on the cross, until He returns for His church, this age, will operate under the same rules that it started with. Therefor there is no reason to disbelieve in the Supernatural being done by Jesus through mankind today, just as it was done in Jesus lifetime. I trust that you will find yourself in the reading of this book.

Through tears and sorrow, through pain and suffering, may the thoughts herein recorded; lead you to victory in Jesus Christ, who alone can give you life, and give it to you more abundantly. John 10:10.

God bless each, and every one of you.

Pastor George Freeman

THE WAR

I lived at home, but I fought the war. For twenty years I lived in a war zone. I was a combat veteran, with post-traumatic stress. My battle hardened heart caused me to fight with neighbors and friends, school teachers and local police. On one occasion I fought hand to hand with a State Trooper. Anyone who irritated me felt my wrath.

The truth be known my war wasn't with them, the war was between my mother and father, I was just the victim of my mother's abusing of my father.

As I reached my teen years the casualties began to mount. First it was just rebellion, later it was taking your wife to the drive-in theater, finally I was to put a loaded handgun to your head. For those who betrayed me the price was high. They might find themselves at the end of a dirt road beaten and broken; or run down with a car and dumped in the brush by the side or the road.

Hate is a powerful, emotion it can drive you to the edge of time; plummet you into the abyss of oblivion! And take you to the gates of hell!

"ALL BEHAVIOR IS LEARNED BEHAVIOR"

"ALL MEN LIVE THE WAY THEIR MOTHER TRAINED THEM"

"ALL WOMEN LIVE THE WAY THEIR FATHER TRAINED THEM"

BUT THERE IS A WAY OUT!

INTRODUCTION

This is not the story of a gang member from Los Angles or the Bronx. George Freeman was not like Ted Bundy; the killer from Alaska or the Green River killer, but his mother was training him just as their mother's had trained them.

He was just a young man as any boy that would be a friend to your son, or who would be interested in your daughter. He was just the boy next door. The young man from down the street. But he had a dark secret, he was full of hate. A genie in a bottle waiting to explode, and he hated women most of all. From the age of five he had been taught to hate; his mother was training him to kill.

The question you are asking me is why would any mother train her son to kill? The next question then is how do mothers teach their sons to hate, and especially to hate women, and to want to kill them?

Well hang around a while and see how his mother did it to him.

You know what the Scripture says. "Train up a child in the way he should go and when he is old, he will not depart from it." Prov. 22:6.

The young George Freeman

THE DAYS OF INNOCENCE BIRTH – 10 YRS.

I was born December 9, 1938. My Father worked for the telephone Co., my mother was a registered nurse. That is how they met. Dad had broken his leg, and mom became his nurse. The rest is history.

We lived in an eight- room house on Mansfield Ave. above the hospital. Dad's bed room was top floor to the right, moms to the left. My bedroom was to the front with a large bathroom to the rear. My favorite room of course was my playroom in the rear on the first floor. We had a large double lot which made a big yard for me to play in. For me everything was wonderful. More toys than I could play with, a very large tree in my back yard to climb, and to fall out of. When I was five years old, I found the cutest girlfriend I had ever had.

Every day in the summer she would come up and we would play until she had to go home. She would say I've got to go home now, and I would say "Lolly, come here I want to tell you a secret", and she would tilt her ear up to me, and I would kiss her. I got away with that all summer, she never caught on.

So, as you can see my life was perfect; at least it was until one particular day when I heard a new sound. I was in the front of the house and heard a lot of yelling and thrashing around in my playroom. Could they be building something new for me? So, I ran down the hall and stopped there in the doorway.

I was scared by what I was seeing. Mom was screaming at dad. She was kicking, slapping, just crazy. She was hurting my dad. I yelled "hitter daddy, hitter daddy", and then I threw my toy rifle at her. Dad bent over to protect her, and the rifle hit him. I turned and ran down the hallway screaming, "I've hurt my daddy, I've hurt my daddy". Unfortunately, the hurting of my father would in time become a way of life with me.

I noticed that they were arguing more and more often. She seemed to be always fussing about something. I don't remember dad ever yelling at her or hitting her, but she always seemed angry.

One day they had a big fight and dad just walked out of the house, got into His car and drove away. I ran to my bedroom and cried. I was so afraid that I would never see my daddy again, I just wanted to die.

By the end of the day he came home he had brought me a brand new two wheeled bicycle, it was a real, big boys, bicycle. What a dad, boy I loved him so much. He put training wheels on it because it was too big for me to balance it. For several weeks I had to use the training wheels, but I was determined to ride it without them, after all I was a big boy now.

They were always good to me. They loved me and brought me everything I wanted. They just couldn't get along with each other.

My dad was my idol, I didn't want to spend much time with my mom. One day I ran away from home. I was probably 7 or 8 years old, I just walked out the door and down the street. I didn't have a plan I just wanted to get away from the storm I guess, I was just looking for peace and quiet.

When I got down into the city a man stopped and offered me a ride. "Where are you going young man"? He asked. I told him I was just running away from home. It turned out that he worked with my dad and he took me to him. I was so happy to see my dad he just loved me and took me back home.

I always felt close to my dad, we just hit it off. He was so smart he just knew everything, just ask him. Everybody loved my dad He was so good to everyone, yet no one wanted to be around my mother, not even her relatives.

In later years some of the family that we hadn't spent time with often, told us why. They said that mom was just too argumentative. That she seemed always on edge, making visits difficult. That is why I never got to know my relatives better.

THE DARK YEARS FROM 10-20 YEARS OLD

I was ten years old when we moved to the country. At 11 a High School girl wanted to show me more about life. At 16 a 28-year- old, married woman got me interested in what she had to offer. I learned to use people to get what I wanted. I learned selfishness that would take me to the gates of hell.

I learned to take care of number one. When people failed me, I taught them the price of betrayal. But all the things I learned from friends, girls, and neighborhood women; paled by comparison to the lessons my mother taught me.

The move from the city to the country at first seemed to me to be a wonderful thing. I was ten years old when we moved. It was a small town about 8-10 miles from the city situated around a good size lake. The lake was about two and a half miles long and a half mile wide.

The Lake was being developed by a few wealthy men including a man called Henry Kendel. He was a manager for movie stars, and vaudeville actors, from New York, city. They built a large restaurant and dance hall at the other end of the lake, where he would bring in the actors every so often. He also developed several, sub-divisions along the side of the lake. My father bought a house in one of them.

The house was a small two bedroom with a full attic which became my playroom. We lived at the entrance to the development off School St. Even being at the top of the hill it was only a fifteen- minute walk to the lake. I was so excited about moving to the country.

I met two other redheaded guys my age and we swam, boated and ran around together all the time. We really didn't look that much alike, but most people thought we were brothers. When people met us by ourselves, they called us Jim or Kidd or George, they didn't know who we were. Kidd had a great speed boat, so we had a fantastic time boating all summer. He also played chess, and we tried our hand at that. Those early years were my best years as being a kid having fun. There was a store with a soda fountain. There was a roller-skating rink at the south end of the lake, and beaches all over the place. At the other end of the lake was a small island, with an old cottage on it. The ground was at water level, so it was wet all the time. We used to boat over to it and play there. No one seemed to know who had owned the island it had been deserted for some time. Between the lake, the friends and the stores, life was peaceful.

UNTIL SHE WALKED IN

When she walked into my life, everything went crazy. She was 16 years old, I was about 11. I had made myself a place in my side yard to play with my toy cars, a little dirt city. I spent a lot of time playing there, I guess it was my quiet place, a place of refuge from the storm.

Then a neighborhood girl strolled into my yard one afternoon. "What are you doing in my yard"? I asked her. She rode the school bus with me. She was several grades ahead of me, but she would never talk to, or even acknowledge me. She always seemed stuck-up, until now. She replied, "I want to show you something that you have never seen before", as she unbuttoned her blouse. "What can you show me that I have never seen before" I said, as I turned to look at her.

Well that look changed my life forever, for the worst. I spent the next 12 years chasing girls instead of learning much at school. Everyone who knows me, knows that I couldn't win a 10 year- old's, spelling contest, if I studied all night; or do simple math, without a calculator.

THE HORSE

When I was about fourteen, dad brought me a horse, but not just any horse this was a palomino show horse. What a dad, my dad was the greatest dad ever. My dad had a friend that lived on the outskirts of a neighboring city, who kept the horse for dad, and taught me to ride. We would go there every Saturday and dad would teach me how to handle her. Dad and I worked on building the barn and the corral for Blondie while he boarded her at his, friends place.

The corral was on a neighbor's property just across the road from the house. There was a stone wall along one side of the corral, where we stacked the manure.

One day Blondie climbed onto the pile and got on the wall and jumped free. We laughed about that for a long time.

The joy of being the owner of a horse, especially a show horse, would soon fade as I found out there was work involved. Feeding her twice each day and grooming her all the time. Dad and I use to groom her together because she would not stand still for me, but he taught her a lesson. One day as he was cleaning her, she reared up on him, so he grabbed her halter as she went up past his head. She was so powerful that she lifted him off his feet. My dad was 6'2" and weighed 260#, but when they came back down his feet hit the ground first. He grabbed her head and flipped her over onto her side laying her on the ground. He just calmly sat on her head and smoked a cigarette. He never had any trouble working with her again.

Dad took control over everything in life. He was a boss where he worked, he saw to it that I did my assigned chores, it was just mom that was out of control.

She ranted and raved, she threw dishes at him, always screaming. Once I saw her dump a pan of hot oatmeal cereal on his head. He just grinned a sheepish grin and finished his breakfast. My pet names for mom were "wild cat", and "spitfire".

Riding the horse was great pleasure she was a five-gated Tennessee Walker. It felt so peaceful to ride her and to get away from all the fuss at home.

Then one day at school a cute red head asked, if I would ever ride my horse to her house? I said I didn't know, then in front of a lot of students she wrapped her arms around my neck and kissed me. I started riding Blondie to her house.

I started taking her riding in a place we called "the pines". It was just a power line cut through a stand of tall pine trees. We would ride a bit together and then I would let her ride by herself. When she road back to me, she would thank me by getting down and we would roll around in the hay hugging and kissing.

One day I road my bike down to her house, I thought we could have more fun if we stayed in the house. I knocked on the door and when she opened it, she looked around for the horse. "Where is Blondie" she asked? "I just bought my bicycle, I thought we could stay here for a change". She just slammed the door in my face. She never even said good-by. She loved my horse, not me. That ended my first big romance.

Outwardly to my friends and at school everything looked great. Away from home I did feel very happy, except for school sports. I hated school sports, because they made each student participate. The team captains would pick students till all were on a team. That was 8th grade for you. I was clumsy, and no one wanted me on their team, so I was most always the last to be picked. I was shamed and just wanted to go home.

Home, did I really want to go home. Home was like living in a war zone. For people that live where shooting is in or about their city it must be horrible. It is not every day maybe, you just never new when she would explode.

We would be sitting at the supper table and she would just start an argument. Before long she would throw a cup of hot coffee in dad's face. "Wildcat". He would just get up and go and sit down in his recliner to read the paper.

That would make her angrier still, she would get up and go over to him and grab the paper out of his hand. The sound of her voice still rings in my ears, "I'm not finished with you yet, Brent" she would scream. "Spitfire." That is the phrase that I remember from her life most.

Most of the time he would just get up, put on his hunting jacket and leave the house.

I would wonder, where did he go, what did he do? I started going with him He went downtown to an old, confectionary store. Where he met three or four other old men to sit and pay cards till 8 or 9 at night. I used to wonder, did their wives drive them out of their houses too? Is this what marriage, is really like?

Dad never badmouthed her to me, I never knew him answer back, or hit her. There was only one thing I can remember him saying. One day as he was teaching me to drive, in what seemed like normal conversation, just one sentence. "When you get married, I am going to leave home." That was it that was all.

He was staying for me. His love for me was so strong that he was taking all that abuse to protect me. He would never abandon me. It was like the old hymn. "Oh, love that will not let me go, I hide my weary soul in thee". The bad side was that the pain in his life was about to get worse.

I BECAME A MAN

The first car I owned was a 1948 Plymouth. It was that military green and I hated it. So, I told dad I was going to paint it light blue. He didn't hold out much hope but said OK. Mom had an Electrolux vacuum cleaner with a moth sprayer attachment; that I planned to use for the paint sprayer. I sanded, puttied and masked the car, in preparation for the painting. Painting was far more work than I had planned for, but dad seemed happy with the results.

THE WOMAN

That year they built a drive-in theater in my area, I got my driver's license and met a woman down by the lake.

Early in the summer I was walking down to the lake one day. In an undeveloped section down toward the lake there was one house being built, and there she sat. "You look so hot and thirsty, let me get you some water." I thought, boy you must really be something for a 28 year- old woman to pay attention to you. She bought out the water, I drank what I wanted, thanked her and went down to the lake.

A few days later I was on the way down to the lake, and there she was again. "I've got something better than water for you come on in." She ran into the house and I followed her. She said, "I'll get you a coke-a-cola."

She got us drinks and led me into her husband's bedroom. We got onto the bed and started to play. I called her tiggly, giggly and wiggly. We had some good laughs and then she popped the question. "My husband works out of town during the week, would you take me to the drive-in every Wednesday night this summer"? I thought, baby I will take you to the moon every night this summer.

I don't know what I told my folks about who I was taking to the drive-in, because they would not have allowed me, to run around with a married woman. I took her to the movies every Wednesday night that summer. There was no sex, just fun. Hugging, kissing and tickling. We just had a great time.

For me the best part was taking her into the concession stand between flicks. To see the wide eyes of my buddy's. They were there with their 14 & 15- year old girlfriends, and me with this wild thing. She hung on my neck, waltzing all around me and kissing me; boy she made me feel 10 feet tall. I hoped this would go on forever; but when the season ended, she disappeared, never to be seen again. She was using me because she was board, no T. V., no radio, no phone.

People ask me, how could you date a married woman? I had been teased by the 16-year old, I had no moral compass and I could never get a date. At the time I never really thought about it.

The stage was now set, all three ingredients were in place. The car to carry out my mission, the power this woman had made me feel, and then there was the hate that roiled within me.

It is hard for a young person to connect the hate that is growing within their heads, with the source of that hate. You seem to have no control over the fits of rage that arise within you, but where does it come from.

From the time I was 15, I had owned a handgun; I had gotten it from a man that owned a gas station. Now having a car, there was a place to keep it. My hate was beginning to bloom. I was getting braver and with a few friends, getting more daring.

With Slug, now in the mix, trouble was inevitable. Stan, we all called him Slug, was very tall 6'6" lean and mean. He really had an even temper, but when pushed he would get crazy. In a gang fight there would be nobody better to have on your side. Once the fight was on, just step back out of the way and slug would finish the job. Something in his head would lock and he would keep swinging till everybody was down. You just had to keep out of his way. I never saw him out gunned.

Now in high school, my rage had reached the boiling point. I would get mad and explode at the slightest provocation. Yet each time I would feel justified, they provoked me, it was their fault. It was always the other guys fault.

You don't understand the undercurrent of rage that is flowing through your mind, as a violent reaction to the way your parents are treating you, or each other. As a young person you live in two different worlds. The world at home, and the world of school, and play. I never saw my outbursts as resentment for what my mother was doing at home to my dad, until 40 years later. By then it was too late.

In high school when someone would knock the books out of my hand, I would explode. The genie would come out of the bottle and we would be into it until one of us was down. During school pictures, a boy pushed me down and got my new suite muddy. I got up and pushed him against the wall until he gave up.

In town one day at the local store, the one that had the soda fountain also had a popcorn machine, I tried to buy a bag of popcorn. You'd put in your dime a bag would slip down and the popcorn would fill your bag. Today the bag did not fall, and the popcorn poured into the waste bin in the bottom of the machine. I was furious, I took some matches, lit them and set the popcorn machine on fire. Of course, the store owner was mad; he put me out of the store and told me to never come back. This was the only store in the area. What was I to do? If a child can't respect his parents, he will disrespect all other authorities.

I waited for several months, and then one night real late, after setting up a good alibi with a friend, I made my move. I took a pry bar and loosened a side window, and slipped in, that was easy. In less than an hour I had trashed the place, even to putting salt and sugar into syrup containers. What a total mess.

The Police went to work and zeroed in on my friend Jim. In fear of jail time Jim told them that it must have been "George", because he got put out of the store. The police did their homework and came for me.

In court I was found guilty, and my father had to pay the cost of repair, along with a heavy fine. I was so sorry, I had embarrassed my dad and hurt him very badly. I just could not stop the crazy in my head. I would try to be good, but then something would set me off and I would be into it again.

This time it was Jim. It took me several months to find out who sicked the cops on me, but it was Jim. When I realized it was him, I got Chazz to help me with the plan. From my 16th year I drove to school in a 53 Ford my dad had gotten for me, so it was real, easy.

One day as Chazz and I were leaving school I noticed Jim just standing waiting for the bus. "Hey Jim, ride home with us", we were laughing and just pretending to be in a real good mood; and he fell for it. He slid into the center between Chazz and I, and we headed for home. We were just joking and having a great time, until I turned onto a dead end, dirt road. At the end of the road we stopped and told Jim to get out of the car. We told him that we knew that he had ratted me out to the cops. He started to beg, he said he had been threatened with jail time, but it was too late to beg. We just left him lying in the dust. They needed to understand that betrayal has its price tag.

The hate that my mother instilled in me by abusing my father for all those years was now bearing fruit. As I felt betrayed by her, so when I was betrayed by others I must respond, with a relentless passion. In this case with Jim I could never let the feel of the betrayal be satisfied. I wanted to strike out at him again and again, and I did. The last time was 3 years later.

I pulled into a restaurant parking lot and noticed Jim's car up in the front. I found a valve stem with a wrench top and walked to his car. No one was around so I loosened all four valves and went back to my car to watch the tires go flat. With- in a very short time Jim and his girlfriend came out to get into the car. "Hey Jim, looks like you have a flat tire" and I just laughed and drove away. I could not forgive, I could not forget, I could not let go. Hate is a very powerful force, but it also sticks in your heart, like poison. It will lead you to the gates of hell.

I always protected those who were loyal to me. My guys knew they could trust and depend on me. One day Jeff and I were driving to meet Pete and when we came upon the sight, we found several guys whipping up on him. I saw one of them coming around his car to get to Pete. I just ran my car right up to his and pinned his legs between the bumpers of both cars. Then I got out and calmed him down. We ran off the others and rescued Pete.

What was so funny, was that I hated bullies, but could not see myself as a bully. Once while I was in the upper grades, I noticed a freshman shoving other kids around. I began to watch and see if he did it very often. He was the brother to a good friend of mine, John. I would need to be very careful, how I handled this situation. In my tactful way I got a small blueberry pie from a concession truck that sold stuff after school. He was standing as the show off in a crowd of students, when I walked up to him. I didn't say anything, I just squashed the pie all over his face. I stood there for a few minutes, then just walked away.

John understood what that was about, so I didn't have any trouble with him, but there would be a reckoning.

Some weeks later John, his brother, a few others, and I went somewhere for a ride. John's brother and I got into an argument while I was driving, so I said, "do you want to stop and talk about it". "Yes" he said, and so we did. We started to fight and ended up in a small stream by the road. I fell on my back in the stream my elbows pinned beneath his knees. A rock the size of a football in his hands. "I'm going to hurt you bad". He said, and but for a dirty little trick that I knew he would have done it. They had to help him to the car. Of, course I would tell you the trick, but you might use it on someone else, and we can't have that can we.

Home, at the end of the day you go home. I don't want you to think that all was bad at home. In fact, the times I spent with my dad were memorable. Besides the horse, we did things together. He liked to fish, and we went out some nights in his rowboat to fish. I didn't care for fishing, but he was always teaching me something. He brought me a 22 rifle and took me into the woods and taught me gun safety and hunting. He would see a squirrel, and tell me how to chase it, and when it was safe to shoot. After the hunt he would show me how to skin and clean them. Then we would, pan fry them and eat them, best food ever. Dad also knew how to trap animals. We made figure 4 stone falls, you can't use them today, but we trapped a lot of rabbits and squirrels. Did you ever eat rabbit stew, yum, yum!

Other people "had to keep up with the Joneses" you know what I mean. Dad had the money, but never felt he had to impress other people. Others at the lake had fancy cars, brought speed boats, and lived in big homes. Dad just felt comfortable in his own skin. With mom always on a rampage, and me always in trouble I could never understand how he just kept putting one foot in front of the other. My dad was the most put together person I had ever met.

My life was like living in three different worlds. The world of reason when I was out with my dad. The world of anger with mom at war, with dad. Then there was the world of fun, crazy fun with the guys.

Sometimes we would drive around at dusk and take turns shooting out people's yard lights. Sometimes we drove around yanking up mailboxes, or just blowing them up with cherry bombs, or just auto racing on the main drag.

One night 5 of my friends went past my house at over 90 miles an hour. They were on School St. a long, straight, level road over a half mile long. Near the junction they lost control, jumped a ditch and rammed a huge tree head first. They left the transmission in the ditch, the car ended up on its nose. Four of them were dead at the scene. That was a very sobering week for me.

Sometimes we would get into gang fights. One time we planned one in a small town. We thought local "yokels" wouldn't know what to make of it. When we showed up to fight, they just brought out the fire truck, and told us to get out of town or get washed down the street. They were smarter than we thought, so we split and laughed about it all night.

The reality though, was that I was just acting tuff to cover the hate that was growing inside my head all the time. I was just venting anger that I was holding against my mother. Now I understand it, but I never realized it then.

One day just joy riding Ralph and I were on a dirt road near the lake. As we started back to the main road three college men came walking toward us. They were side by side in the center of the road. I told Ralph to lock the doors. We stopped, and they surrounded the car and told us to get out, that they were taking the car. I told them that we were going on down the road and the man in front of the car needed to move. They laughed, and I stepped on the gas. The fellow leaned over the hood of the car, and I took him on down the road. When we got to the main road, I just locked up the brakes and he went flying into the bushes across the road. We just went merrily on our way.

There seemed to be always some trouble to get into even when I didn't expect it. I was just leaving school, one day, and horsing around a bit with the car, maybe driving a little fast. I noticed a car coming toward me, the man motioned with his hand for me to stop or slow down. It was not a police car, he wore no uniform, so I kept going. In a flash he was in reverse and keeping along side of me. So, I gunned it and took off. I watched him wheel around and chase after me. Well I flew, turning left then right, going through stop signs, and lost him. Did he think he was as good as me? I showed him. That unnerved me but I'm the best car handler in town. Maybe not the smartest as the next day would prove, but I could wheel a mean machine.

The following day was cool, but when I got home and pulled into my driveway, He was sitting there waiting for me. A detective, oh boy am I in trouble, I needed to think fast. I began to beg and plead. "Please don't tell my father, he will take my license away for six months." I cried, I ran snot, I pleaded, and it worked. I promised to never drive crazy again. He let me go.

Every time when I went before a judge, I would play the same act. They would say "I am going to be merciful this one time." I would promise, "I will never do wrong again". When I got outside the courthouse, I would laugh at them, and go back to my old ways.

One time I shot an arrow into someone's upper window, just for fun. You know we were crazy. This was a release from the tension of my home life. It got to the point that I found myself in the police station several times a month.

J. Edger Hoover, said those brought up in church, are rarely brought up in court. I wish mom had known that.

Then I met a guy that had a very risky idea. "Let's just go joy riding with some very nice cars."

We would drive around till we found one. My buddy would jimmy the door and hot wire the car. They would take off and we would meet at a predetermined place. I would leave my car and we would just drive around, enjoying our new wheels. Sometimes we would even find one in a dealership and take it for a ride. When we took plates for the cars, sometimes we had to get plates off the backs of two cars, because of how they were parked.

It was fast getting to the point that the law was getting serious in its demands to shut me down. One night a State police officer stopped in the front yard to look at the dents in my car fender. He said he believed I had been in a hit-n-run accident that day, and he arrested my on the spot. When he tried to get me into the cruiser I refused to go, and the fight was on. I believe he could have gotten me into the car, but he was too decent a man to use mace or his night stick. My father came out and told me to go with him, that he would come up and bring me home. We won that case in court but there were those we did not. Eventually a Judge gave my father a choice; a small jail sentence or send George to a reform school. Dad chose reform school.

Munson Academy, in Munson, Mass. A whole summer, are you kidding? There were about 60 other boys there. Of course, there were classrooms and dorms, a big kitchen with a dinning, hall. We were under strict rules of behavior, and every hour we had to be on the grounds. Everything was regulated, a time for class, a time for meals, and lights out sack time. The only freedom we had was a few hours a few times a week to go to town to buy anything we needed. If we got on probation by breaking rules, you lost those privileges. There was a bowling alley and girls there that liked bad boys; and we spent much of our free time there. It amazes me that no one suspected that I was now in a group of likeminded bad guys.

In high school my attitude continued to worsen, there was such rebellion that I had lost all respect for myself, I just didn't care anymore. Let them get out of my way or get run over. I remember taking all the screws out of the desk I was sitting in during class. I stood out in the hall to watch the boy in the next class throw his books onto the desk. It just disintegrated all over the floor. Who me I was just watching. I just got into trouble all the time, which led to the big one.

Two weeks before Christmas, in my senior year I was guarding the boy's restroom. At noontime after lunch some of the boys would go into the restroom to smoke. Of course, this was against the rules; rules, rules, we hated rules. This was my turn to be the guard. I would just stand at the corner with my leg bent up on the wall. Any time a teacher would come my way I would just put my leg down and walk away.

Today the teacher grabbed me and said that I was going to the Principals office for guarding the boy's restroom. I said I wasn't doing any-thing and I wasn't going to go anywhere with him. And the fight was on. After we scuffled a while, he took me to the Principal. They concluded that I needed time off to decide if I wanted to further my education.

They sent me home and told my father that I could come back next year if I promised to obey the rules. My father was really angry, he got me a job at the American Thread Co.

My job was running a thread stretching machine on the midnight shift, I didn't like that. Dad was dead serious, I had to work there until school started the next year. It was hot, dirty and noisy. Not many people on the third shift, so it would be inevitable that I would get into trouble. Sometimes the machine would run out of thread, or I would not cut the tangles. Once when they were dying thread, I let the vat overflow for an hour and the dye dripped down three floors. Sometime the dye ran too slow and half the spools came out white. I don't know why they didn't fire me.

I did not know it at the time but all the trouble I got into, and all the pain I was causing my father was the results of the anger I felt toward mom. What hurts me the most even to this day is that I was doubling his pain. Not only did he have an abusive wife, but he also had a troublesome kid. Pain upon pain. I couldn't stop hurting him because I couldn't stop hating her.

When I was 19, after all those years of watching her abuse dad, I used to lay in bed thinking, I am going to rape her, stab her to death and burn the house down around her. Someone said, "You don't know what goes on behind closed doors", but their door was never closed.

Once when I was 11 years old and dad had gone to work all night. She called for me, and now at 19 the thoughts of that night made me hate her even more. If you think of evil long enough, you will give in to it. You would even kill. If you raise your child in evil, he may become the evil you raised him to be.

THE DARKNESS FADES

In all the world, and of all the people that have ever had an impact on my life there is one man that stands out. He stands head and shoulders above the rest. I am not comparing him to my dad for there is no one to fill that place. Yet the Resident State Trooper; Officer Kolodziej, was very responsible for my turn around. He kept working on me, "how can I help you, George"? He would ask.

Day after day, week after week and month after month, he was as a friend to me. Every time that I was brought into the police station, he treated me with dignity and respect. I have been slammed around in a police station, and by the Chief of Police, in another station but not by him. No yelling, no threats, no intimidation just as a father pity's his children, he was incredible.

One of the last times I would be in his office, he would write me out a warning. So, I asked him what I needed to do with it, show it to a Judge. No just keep it, but I rolled it up into a ball and through it in his face and walked out. My guys said, "Are you crazy", he came right up and over his desk. I didn't appreciate the man he really was, till I met Jesus Christ.

The Chief had done all he could as a human being to help me. He had done more than any reasonable person could or would do, but he was at his wits end. He had tried and failed, but who hadn't.

He and his wife were going to a little country church, in a neighboring town. A small country Baptist Church. The church was pastored by, a young, newly married minister. As a last resort the Chief talked to his Pastor about me and asked him to help me.

Mean, while Satan had one more whack at me. This would be a mean one.

I was 19 at the time, and to drink at a bar you had to be 21. I decided to alter my draft card to show my age at 21. Just a 10- year prison term if you get caught. Then me and a buddy started taking our dates to big city clubs for drinking and dancing. The girls loved it, and it really built my ego, as if that needed to be done.

As time would pass something would go wrong. Everything seemed fun until one night after a few hours of drinking and dancing a sailor wanted to dance with my girl. What got me mad was, that she enjoyed it more than when she and I were dancing.

I said, "Let's get out of here". We got up and went out to the car. The sailor came out with us, talking with my girl. We all got into the car, but she rolled down the window. He stuck his head into the open window talking with her and tried to steal a kiss. That was it that was all I could take, I reached into the glove box and pulled out the handgun. I always kept it loaded.

I put the barrel of the gun right on his head and told him that I would blow him away if he did not get out of my sight. He must have believed me because he disappeared. The truth is that I would have done it if he hadn't gone. Later that night I fell apart thinking about the electric chair. Thank God that I didn't kill him, because in a few weeks my life was going to change for ever.

THE DAWN

It was a day like any other. It was in the fall maybe, October, I can't say for sure. It was after school and I was walking through the dinning; room when the phone rang. I stopped and picked up the phone.

A man on the other end asked, "Is this George Freeman?" "Yes" I said. He continued "I am the Pastor, of the DePot Baptist Church. Would you be willing to go to a Youth for Christ meeting this coming week-end?" I answered yes. He made the arrangements to pick me up at the appointed time and said good- by, and I hung up the phone.

As I stood there scratching my head, I said to myself "you're crazy". Why would you want to go to church? I really felt out of it. Church is for losers. I can handle life all by myself, I don't need any help. I've got it all together, right, yah right.

I don't remember anything that was said or done at the meeting. I was surprised by what I saw. The girls were better looking than I would have expected.

I thought that the only people that went to church were losers, people that couldn't make it on their own. Those that were plain, homely, or crippled, I was none of those, I was great, I didn't need any help, I could make it on my own.

Then my eyes focused on a guy, he was a guy that I knew from high school, "Jack". In school he didn't seem to be a religious nut, he was a little square, but not churchy. Still I thought that this church stuff might not be as bad as I had thought. I should at least give it a try, after all how bad could it be? What could it hurt? Jack, and I hit it off right away.

At the church, I met another family that was very easy to like. My mother worked on Sundays as a nurse in a convalescent home. Dad needed the day to rest from work; mom, and me. The James's invited me to their house for dinner every Sunday after church. They were a very warm family, and really showed me love.

The James's lived on School St. just down the road from my place. The huge tree that my friend's car hit the night they got killed, was on their property. Lois and Francis had at least four children. The oldest was a girl about my age. Some evenings I would go and visit with her. Her mother would go to bed early and we would watch T.V. together, it was nice.

I had been going to church now for about three months since I had put the gun in that sailor's face. I didn't understand it much, I had never read the Bible, or been in a church like this one. I really liked the Pastor and all the people were very kind to me. I just had never heard that the Bible was true, that God was real. The only thing that I could remember from before, was a conversation between a girl and her youth Pastor "How can we believe in the virgin birth?" His reply "I don't know we just have to believe."

THE VISITATION

The Pastor would preach his sermon, after the singing. Then he would have the congregation stand, and he would ask if anyone wanted to come forward for prayer. This was always the way they did every service; Sunday morning, Sunday evening and Wednesday evening, it was always the same.

This, particular; Sunday morning started as usual. The Pastor preached his message and asked us all to stand for the closing prayer. That was just as usual, but in five minutes, nothing in my life would ever be usual again.

Slowly but surely something powerful began to come down over my being. It is hard to describe. It was like nothing I had ever felt before; scary, comforting, and like liquid electricity, the most awesome feeling ever.

I began to tremble, shake, and cry. No one seemed to notice they just left the church and went on their way, as usual.

The Pastor and I were all alone. I stood there for a few minutes in the silence, then he asked," what is happening to you George?" "I was hoping that you could tell me?" I said. "Do you really want to know" he asked. "Yes," I answered. In a few minutes the feeling lifted, and I began to calm down. I had been enraptured by love.

This was the first, of three times in my life that there would be a Divine visitation of God into my life's situations. When people try to tell me that all manifestations of the Holy Spirit were only for the first century, they are talking to the wrong person. Any time God wants to step into your life he can and will.

MY NEW LIFE IN CHRIST

That Tuesday I went to the parsonage, so he could tell me what was happening. He told me that I was a sinner, I didn't have any problem believing that. He told me that Jesus was the Son of God, and that he had died for my sins. All I had to do was to repent of them and ask Him to be the Lord of my life.

He took me down the Roman road. It was there for me to see for myself, there in the New Testament. There in the book of Romans, Romans 10:9-11. "That if you shall confess with your mouth the Lord Jesus and shall believe in thine heart that God has raised him from the dead, you shall be saved. For with the heart man believeth unto righteousness; and with the mouth confession is made unto salvation. For the Scripture says, "Whosoever believeth on him shall not be ashamed." He led me in a prayer of repentance, and commitment. Then he prayed God's blessing over me, and said now you are saved, and a child of God. We hugged and I started for home.

That is when the problem started. I know now it was the Devil whispering in my ear "you are too bad He didn't forgive your sins."

You see that Sunday was so powerful to me, and today there were no feelings at all. I just thought that I was worthless, and He didn't want me, and I cried most of the way home. I was to find out that it's not about feelings, it's about; that God is true to His word, if He says it, He will do it. We can depend on God, all the Time.

When I got home, I was alone, and I just sank into my dad's recliner. That's when it happened. That's when the most incredible peace came over me. I had always been restless, but now I was at rest and I said to myself. The war is over.

It was really true I had been enveloped in a love that I could not explain, but it was like being wrapped up in something warm and protective.

THE WAR IS OVER

The one thing I have been able to say from that day to this, is that I have never had to be entertained. I don't need TV., games, sports, or anything to be fulfilled, I am content. My life in Christ Jesus had now begun. My rebirth date was the week of February 10, 1959. Wow! "The peace that passes understanding." Phil. 4:7.

Now I could start living, the joy was overwhelming. Every day was so exciting. I was learning new things and meeting new people all the time. It seemed that God had decided to pour out the Holy Spirit upon our church without even telling us about it. Acts 2:4.

I was water baptized and filled with the Holy Ghost evidenced by speaking with other tongues. New gifts and ministries began to flow and operate. We would see them in the Bible and then they would start happening. Some were Speaking in tongues, some were Prophesying, I felt like laying hands on people as I was led of the Spirit. When I moved out as I felt the Spirit it would work, but if I waited nothing seemed to happen.

I felt very close to the Pastor; He and I visited the sick and went to the hospitals together often. I spent a lot of time with him. Sometimes we talked for hours after church. Maybe once a month we would visit his Uncles church on a Sunday afternoon. There were brothers that pastored country churches. Their father had felt to open empty church buildings and give one to each of his sons to pastor. I never met the other brother.

His uncle was the Pastor of an old country church. The church was past Lake Haywood, we called it Lake Waywood, because the people were swimming there on Sundays.

Where Pastor brought gas, the station owner asked him to visit his wife. They were in their 50's. She had, had a mental break down and she was in the hospital.

He asked me to go with him. In the visitation room they brought her to our booth. She shuffled her feet, she held her arms tight to her body, with her hands clubbed inward and her head down on her chest.

She sat down and talked to us in a man's voice. "What do you want with me"? Pastor talked to her for a few minutes, but she did not look up or respond at all. He read to her from his Bible for a few minutes and she began to open- up to him.

First, she lifted her head and began to smile. Then she opened her arms and put them on the table. As he continued to read the Bible to her, she opened her hands and seemed visibly relaxed.

He closed the Bible and talked with her for a few minutes and she responded in a sweet feminine voice. As the time past she began to revert to her original position. She pulled her arms to her body, clubbed her hands and talked to us in a man's voice. "I've got to go now". She turned and shuffled away.

I just marveled that reading Gods word had that much power to control a demon. Watching that shivered me to the bone. Would she have been set free if we had known then what we know now?

MINISTRY

I just thought that going with my Pastor was normal. Then he told me that he believed that I was being called to the ministry. I asked, "What was that"? I had never for a moment thought of where ministers came from, or about me being one. I was just lost in the wonder of watching God do everything that He was doing now.

He said that I needed to go to Bible school. He said that there was one in a nearby state. He mentioned that they were different than we were, but that I could trust them. I made application with Zion Bible Institute, for the fall of 1959, and began to talk with dad about it.

Dad was not enthused. After the lifestyle I had been living I could not blame him. He had tried church years before and the experience had left him cold. That church was just a religious thing, teaching people to be good, and my dad was good.

We left the discussion that if I decided to go, they would take me up there, but that I would have to stay. He said that I could not come home for Christmas. As I waited on God, I felt no peace in my heart, and so I finally told them that I wanted to go. I packed my stuff and they drove me to Zion. We said good- by and he reminded me that I could not come home.

ZION

Zion Bible Institute had been started by a couple from Brazil, in South America. Rev. Christine Gibson, born in 1878, and her husband felt led of the Lord to come to America and start a convalescent home for older folks. They had several acres of land and built a church on the property. Sadly, the first church service would be a funeral service for her husband.

I don't know when they had the first thoughts of adding a Bible school to the mix, but in the fall of 1924, they held their first graduation. She went to be with the Lord in 1955. The school and the church, Zion Gospel Temple, then came under the leadership of the Rev. Dr. Leonard W. Heroo, her prodigy.

in Zion

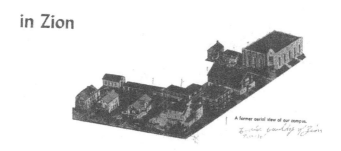

A former aerial view of our campus.

I settled into the routine of classes, meeting new people and the new surroundings. It was all very exciting, and intensely spiritual; it was powerful. The school was a faith school, and as such they did not charge me to come there to study, eat and live. There was just a small tuition fee.

The teachers had room and board, but no guaranteed salary. To see their sacrifice, and manor of life was an incredible example to me. They showed great love and concern for each other and for all the students. They lived what they preached.

Christmas that first year was a mixture of joy and sorrow. I missed home, but there was the time I spent alone on Christmas day. There was a few staff and students that were there, so we ate together, but most of the day I spent in my room. I picked up a Hymn book and began to read it page by page. As I read each Hymn and tried to sing them, I realized that I only, new a few. I could not believe that there were so many hymns. Has I read, sang and praised through tears; I saw that Jesus was much more powerful and loving than I had ever realized before. I was just beginning to experience the love of God.

The teachers lived on the grounds, in small apartments. The Students 4 to a room in dorms, with bathrooms down the hall. We all ate in the dinning, hall together. We had 2 classes and chapel before lunch then 2 classes before supper. Each student had assigned duties besides keeping your room clean. Chapel was always exciting. Sometimes the principle spoke, a teacher, or a student, sometimes it was funny, but it was always good. There was singing and worship and gifts of the Holy Spirit. You never knew what would happen.

LOSING DAD

In the second year at Zion, my father died. I had gone home for Christmas, but they hid from me that he had cancer. So back in school in late January I was called home, dad was in the hospital. He died in early February. I have always wished that he had met Sandy, he would have loved her too. Mom and I took turns sitting with him in the hospital. I stayed during the day and mom watched dad at night. One night about 3:00 a.m. I was awakened by voices as mom walked around the house to the front door. I thought to myself that mom wouldn't be home if dad was still alive. It was a very tuff time in my life, but I was comforted by a car load of my roommates from Zion; God is so good.

Losing my father was like losing the only stability I had ever known. Dad was my rock. He was always on my side, always in my corner. When I had gotten in trouble with the law, he walked through it with me. He did not condone my actions, but I felt that he always tried to understand me. He did not beat me when I got arrested, he just stood quietly beside me. Mom was a storm dad was my shelter from the storm. Please understand they were not permissive parents, I had duties and if I didn't do them, I was punished. I didn't like mowing the lawn, so one time I cut down some of mom's flowers. I thought maybe they would get someone else to mow the lawn, instead I got a spanking. Dad always showed that he was proud of me when I did something good.

When I customized my first car, a 48 Plymouth. I installed an old Buick grill and frenched the headlights. Then I decided to paint the car a light blue, it had been that ugly military green. The old Electrolux vacuum cleaner had an attachment that sprayed moth stuff and I thought that I could paint the car with it. Dad just shook his head and went to work, but I started masking and painting. When he got home that night he beamed, he just could not believe how great it looked. He just made me feel super, he always did. Now I would need to find out that Jesus would become my rock, if I would let Him. That would be the test. With all my failures, I would find Jesus would always surpass the test.

SANDY

Zion gave me three things: The power in the Holy Ghost, a sound foundation in God's word and Sandra June Maze. I called her "Dusty". She was like a soft summer breeze.

While other girls were trying to show off their talents or getting noticed by the boys; she was just there to find the will of God for her life. She was quiet and soft spoken; she was just there. I can't remember the first time I saw her, but what I do remember was that she was unassuming. I remember her spending time in the prayer room. I began, to notice her about the campus, her easy manner.

I had always been the center of attraction; others stole cars, I stole only "fancy ones" In the gang I carried the gun, I was always the loudest squeak in the wheel. She could live without being the center of attention. She seemed so real, so Christ like. We all had a duty to perform each week, some wined and complained she just quietly did her task.

I remember, siting, next to her once at lunch time. We had assigned seats, but sometimes George would fudge the rules. Honey, could you please pass me the butter?" She had to deal with that. She thought he's getting too serious. She said, "I just want to be friends." "Me to" I responded. That calmed her heart. Years later I told her, the kind of friends that wanted to get married.

She could be offended, but not strike back. She could be hurt by the misdeeds of others yet be forgiving. Her roommate would borrow her clothes and other things, only to return them dirty, damaged or not at all. Even when she had to scrub them to get them clean, or throw them away, she never retaliated or became bitter, she cried, but she always forgave. A Proverbs 31, woman.

I don't know how it started; I just remember us going together. We started walking around the grounds. We started eating together, talking together; just spending time together. The school didn't allow student dating, we were required to always be in groups, especially in public.

In her third year the school opened a fellowship hall. It was much needed because boys and girls of marital age will find a way to get together. The hall was a place to eat and have fun talking with others. Weekdays it was open after supper, but on Saturday it was open all day long. We spent many good times there. Some Saturdays we had breakfast or another meal there, it was cozy.

EXPERIENCE

During one of the summer breaks, a group of Zion students were given the opportunity to run a kid's camp.

I was just one of the councilors. It was the most exciting thing I had ever done. We had great church services, and the alter times were just out of sight. But the kids just wouldn't settle down at night. What to do? The man running the camp said to us don't worry about that I'll take care of it. So one night about 3 o'clock he got us up and we dragged the kids out of bed and onto the sports field and gave them an hour of calisthenics. They seemed more willing to go to bed on time after that. We all had a great time that camp.

There was one special moment for me. There was one boy that would not eat his meals well but was always eating candy during the day. So, one morning I sat next to him at breakfast. I told him that he needed to finish his food, he just laughed at me. When the bell, rang and all the other kids got up I kept him in his seat. Finish your breakfast, I said. "No" he replied. So, I kept him there for about half an hour. He ate a few more bites and cried. He said, "Grand ma doesn't make me eat, I am going to tell my father when he comes Saturday."

When his father came, I was nearby and heard him say. "Take me home he is mean to me." His father asked what did he do. The boy answered, "He makes me eat all my food." GOOD said his father I am going to sign you up for the second week.

BACK IN SCHOOL

In my second year I was able to go to "outside ministry". Some churches would invite the students to come and minister at their church. This would give us the opportunity to develop our gifts, and talents. We went with a teacher. The girls usually sang, and the boys preached.

I used to wonder, what hillbillies eat? So, on one outside trip, they served us sandwiches. The choice was chicken salad or lobster salad. My choice of course was lobster, but she would never eat it, it was so disgusting looking. I switch her chicken salad for a lobster salad sandwich, when she wasn't looking. As she finished the first half I asked, "How did it taste?" "It was great" she said. "That was lobster" I said. I had to get her a Chicken sandwich. To this day, 60 years later she does not like real seafood.

That day after I was introduced to preach, the Spirit told me to wait. Then another student gave a prophecy. Then I read my text and again the Spirit told me to wait, and another person gave another message, then I was released to preach.

Sandy and I got engaged during my second year, her third year. Sometimes on outside ministry a group of students would come to my church in the DePot. They would sing and preach, I made sure she would be in that group. That's how Sandy met mom, and we got engaged. I brought her a hope chest and kept it in my dorm room at Zion. It's still with us here to this day.

When I went to visit Sandy at her house her father would not let me stay on the farm. Her Pastor, Rev. Olan Knotts, let me stay in the evangelist apartment in the church. He was a very dedicated man of God. That summer I helped her dad clear 5 acres of land. I thought that it would help him to get to like me, it didn't.

I went home some weekends to visit my local church. Some time in my second year of school, the church changed Pastors. I never did know how that came about, but he felt that he had an apostolic calling. That his mission was to set the church in order. They were very spiritually minded and extremely dedicated to the Lord. They came to us from a Bible school called "Bethany"; where they met Rev. David Ferrero.

THE CONVENTION

Meanwhile back in my last year at Zion, we went to a convention in the North Country. The churches in that county sent a whole railroad car full of potatoes to the school every year. So, in the spring the school sent a group of students with a teacher to minister at their convention. It was a wonderful time for me. I had never seen anything like this, it was a whole weeklong, three services a day. Such singing, worship and preaching. It was awesome.

One afternoon I was scheduled to preach, so after lunch I went upstairs in the men's dorm to pray. While reading the Bible I heard someone start up the stairway. The Holy Spirit spoke clearly to my spirit. "He's going to ask you how you baptize, tell him in water". I thought, "I'm not getting into this", so I got up and moved to the end bunk and turned my back to the room. I bent over the Bible and told the Lord "I am not going to say that".

When that guy got to the top of the steps, he came toward me, but set down on a bunk about four bunks from mine. He was quiet for a while, but then he asked; "how do you baptize?" I just swung around and said, "In water".

He exploded and said. "The Lord told us you have to be baptized in Jesus name before, you can get the Holy Ghost". I told him that that is not true, and showed him in the Scripture, in Acts 10: 44-48. Where the Holy Ghost fell on the people before they were baptized in Jesus name. He got mad and went back down stairs. I didn't understand all that, but at least I was learning to understand when God was speaking to me.

On another occasion, I was studying in my dorm room, after lights out, and the Dean of men asked why we were still up. Then he asked another student, what should you say when you baptize someone? He said. "In the name of the Father, the Son and the Holy Ghost." The Dean, responded, "The disciples said, "in the name of Jesus". The student replied, "I don't care what the disciples did I am going to do what Jesus said", and the Holy Spirit said to me, "The disciples did what Jesus said, only you don't understand it." It would be some time before I would have the understanding that you just can't use one verse of Scripture to prove a point.

BACK HOME

Sometime in the early spring of 1962, we would be introduced to Rev. David Ferrero. Pastor Ferrero was from the State of Washington, he just fit right in with us. He was a good Bible teacher and a very humble man, and soon became our Pastor. He was single when he came, but he would meet a young lady named "Joan".

I have always liked David; he was so easy to be around.

Once when I was in from school; I was just greeting the saints, as I walked into church. I passed a new face and as I said hello to him, the Spirit said "Diakoneo." I thought that's a weird name, but I continued up to the platform, to greet David. I told him what the Spirit had said and ask him if that was that man's name. David just laughed, and told me that, that was the Greek word for deacon. He said the man was a deacon from another church and was just visiting.

On another occasion a man came to us from another State. He told us that the Lord had said for him to join our church. The Spirit spoke to me and said, "I did not tell him to come here, he is running away from a situation, tell him to go back home."

This was the first of many times that God would give people direction through a word of knowledge or a prophecy by me. I was very nervous about this, but I went ahead and spoke it out to this man.

He said, that he didn't know what I was talking about, that I was wrong. He went to the rear of the church to the Pastor and asked David "do you believe his prophecy"? David answered, "I don't know about the prophecy, but I believe in George." It was unnerving but three weeks later he slid into the seat next to me and said that I had been right and that he was going to go back home and deal with the issue. I was glad for him.

SPRING BREAK

Sandy and I had planned to marry on June 2nd two days after my graduation. I was going to go down to her house on Spring break to ask her father's permission for his daughter's hand in marriage. This goal of marrying the girl of my dreams was so exciting that I still don't know how I kept up my grades. At the break I went down to West Virginia.

I was there a few days to get my nerve up. Her mother and Sandy both knew why I had come, but when I told them that I was going in to ask Sant at that moment, they both ran into their bedrooms to hide. Well that didn't calm my nerves any. What would happen to me now, was he going to explode? Still this must be done,

So, I slipped into the living room, and sat down. He was reading the paper, he never stopped or looked up. I just took a breath and began. You know Sandy and I met in school and I fell in love with her. We have planned to marry. I have come here now to ask your permission to have your daughter's hand in marriage. He replied, "You are both over 21 and don't need my permission." "Yes sir." I said, "But we would like to have it." Dead silence, then he grunted.

That was it that was all. I thought I would pass out, but I got up and went into the kitchen. Sandy and her mom came into the kitchen, but there was no celebration, just restrained joy. Oh, what a relief it was.

BACK TO THE BOOKS

I was glad to get back to school. At Zion I dug into my studies, with my heart pounding, counting every day. Mom gave me money to buy a new car for the wedding. So, I asked the principle for permission to buy one. They O.K. it, and I found a beautiful, Plymouth fury convertible. Robin's egg blue, it made the eyes roll at school. It didn't look quite like a preacher's car.

While I was basking in the sunlight of love Sandy was working hard on her wedding plans; getting gowns, sending invitations, picking her ladies. I had asked my roommate Harry Rideout to be my best man, so my part was covered. We planned a two week honeymoon up into Canada. To Niagara Falls, the thousand Isles, Sturbridge Village and to end up on Cape Cod.

GRADUATION/WEDDING

You want to talk about nerves, I'll show you nerves. Classes are finished, and your class is practicing for a very large and grandiose graduation ceremony and all you can think of is your wedding ceremony. The graduation will be held in Zion Gospel Temple, at the school. The temple seats 1,200 people, and it will be full. There will be several days of special speakers and the graduation on Wednesday.

Then you drive to West Virginia Thursday. Friday night you do the wedding rehearsal. The Pastor says to Sandys dad, "Aren't you glad to get your daughter married?" Sant said, "I never did want my kids to leave home". We all held our breath.

Saturday afternoon about 2:00p.m. Shaking to the bone, we take our places in the front of the church, with the Minister. The, Rev Leon Brassfield, was a new minister to that church. This was his first wedding.

THE WEDDING

Sandy looked so beautiful, just like an angel in her gown. The wedding went off without a hitch until the closing prayer. He finished the prayer saying, "May they rest in peace". Then he must have realized what he had said and added "In peace with you Lord." (swak) sealed with a kiss. Praise be to the Lord.

We all seemed to relax and rejoice. We all hugged each other and started toward the farm. We celebrated all afternoon with food, fun, and lots of pictures. Then we all went inside to open the gifts. Wow what a day. This day would be only eclipsed by the honeymoon.

THE HILLBILLY AND THE HELICOPTER

The honeymoon was more wonderful than I could have possibly imagined. The sights, the Falls, the fancy foods, it was all too wonderful. Our first times alone together was beyond anything I could have dreamed of.

On the other hand, Sandy had never been swimming, so getting Sandy into a swimsuit and into the water; that was something else, she was so nervous. We still have the swimsuit.

Then we found that we could go up over the Falls in a helicopter, I said to myself that will never happen; but she got right in and off we went. A hillbilly in a helicopter who, would believe it. The Cape was so unbelievable, sun, sand and surf. It was breath taking. Basking in the sun, quaint little shops, life was good.

With a grand finally, at Sturbridge Village.

MARRIED LIFE

All good things come to an end and you have, to go home. Going home was fine, except mom would be there. The plan was to have been; that mom was to move to an apartment at the convalescent home, where she was the nurse, in Stafford Springs. You know they say, "The plans of mice and men go astray."

So, it would come to pass that the three of us would spend several weeks living together, very interesting. One time, mom took the flat iron out of sandy hand and said, "That's not how to iron my boy's pants", Oh- no! Mom!

We needed to be on our own, so we rented an apartment from the church, and Moved.

Sandy, and I, settled into our married life. We were still going to the church with David now the Pastor. I was trying to find work and to find my place in the body of Christ there. How could I fit all the pieces together; new believer, new husband, employee, minister trainee, Prophet. Boy oh boy, is growing up tuff.

Can I suggest to you, that you listen to me, and do each of these one at a time. It would have been easier on Sandy, on me, on everybody if I had.

I was able to get work in Benny's Auto Store, assembling bikes and being a, floor salesmen, for $ 120.00 a week. Yes, the Lord, is gracious to help those who can't seem to help themselves. All down through the years I have found that Jesus really watches over you, watches over all of us. Praise be to the Lord.

THE HOLY SPIRIT

We were in the early years of what was called "The Charismatic movement". In the early 1900's the Azusa Street Revival produced the largest moving of the Holy Spirit since Pentecost. It was responsible for the birth of Pentecostal church's world- wide. Sometime in the middle of the Century the Holy Spirit began to fall on the old main-line churches.

I would not have known this until years later. All we knew was that something wonderful was happening. We knew that it was the Baptism in the Holy Spirit, so we just gave ourselves to it. Yes, we stumbled along, but Jesus loved us in our baby steps. In those early years I experienced; Tongues, interpretation of tongues, Prophecy, healings and casting out demons.

In the mid to late 60's, the presence of God had become so powerful that students from the University of Conn., and even people from out of State, came to see for themselves. One student, Mike Josiah, a Jewish boy, accepted Jesus as his savior and messiah. I baptized him in December at the lake, what a joy that was for me. Others were being saved and being baptized in the name of the Lord, also.

There were many fine times in the natural as well. David and Joan got married. Sandy was pregnant, and in the manner of time our first son was born. One day I came home from work as usual and looked, into the kitchen. I could see a note on the kitchen table, but I went into the bedroom and took off my clothes and rested for a while. I thought the note might have said that she had gone shopping with mom.

Eventually I went into the kitchen meaning to go into the bathroom and I stopped to read the note, which read. Hurry, the baby is coming. I dressed and raced to the hospital, just in time to see Sandy just before they wheeled her into delivery.

We called the baby Nathan, because that was the name of his Jewish doctor. At the last minute the doctor had felt to have one more x-ray and discovered that the baby had turned around, and was, frank breach. If they had not known this the birth might have been dangerous to Nate. Praise the Lord. Nathan was born July 11th 1963.

THE PROPHET, BILL BRITAIN

In the spring of 1964, I had a dream about Abraham leaving his home country and moving to another country. It seemed very real and to have a spiritual meaning. It caused me to build a trailer on an old truck Frame and load our stuff and head out.

I believed we should go to visit the Prophet Bill Britain, in Springfield, Mo. We left the trailer and somethings at Sandys home in West Virginia and proceeded toward Springfield. We had purchased, a brand- new Plymouth, a four- door sedan.

On a Sunday near Springfield I noticed the oil light come on. I stopped to check the oil and found it very low. I thought the car's oil pan might have been damaged on the rough terrain on Sandy's farm.

I pulled into the next gas station I came to and ask if they would check the oil pan. When they lifted the car up, they found that the oil sending unit had gone bad and was leaking. This, was a brand, new car, and on a Sunday, what can we do? The station owner went to his cash register and opened it up and pulled out a brand new, oil sending unit. Unbelievable; that's right. That might have been a small miracle, but a miracle none the less. He installed the unit and the new oil we paid him and off we went.

THE PROPHET

Bill Britain, there is way too much to tell about this man of God. I have never met a man so naturally supernatural as Bill Britain, before or since. To him, being in the Spirit was just like water running off a duck's back. When he felt that God spoke to him about building him a church in Springfield. He just called the operator and she got him a realtor. He told him I print literature and need a large dry basement, four bedrooms and a large empty attic. They had the house that Bill, needed. He was like Paul the Apostle.

When they needed a bedroom set, he saw an auction sign, and felt that the Spirit told him to stop and go to the auction. Going up the driveway he heard the auctioneer saying "$ 3.00 once, $3.00 twice", and felt that the Spirit said, "Bid. Bill yelled $4.00 and the auctioneer said "sold". Bill ran around the corner and asked, "What did I buy?" The people all laughed. It was the bedroom set they wanted.

While I was there, he was showing me the picture of a bookbinding machine he needed for making thick books. Bill had been in the printing ministry for many years and had a mailing list of around 8,000. A new machine cost $10,000.oo, even a used one was $6,000.oo.

A few weeks, latter, when I got to the house there was a nice yellow station wagon in the driveway. It had California plates on it and a large box inside. When I got inside the house the man was telling Bill that he felt that the Lord told him to buy it for Bill and take it to him. It was the new bookbinding machine that Bill needed.

When we were in Springfield, it had not rained for a long time and the river -beds were almost dry. Bill announced one day the date for their camp meeting.

They owned a few acres of land that they called Sacred Acres Campground. One of the ministers had been in SAC in the Airforce. When we arrived for the week of camp, we were told that there was no water, that the well was empty, and the springs were dry. At the first service after the meeting we all prayed for rain. It rained all night, and in the morning, we were told that the well was full; and the springs were running water.

We had a great week of camp, but as we drove back to Springfield, we noticed that it hadn't rained anywhere except at the campground. It was always like that with Bill Britain. No matter what, he just quietly flowed in the Spirit.

Our second son was born there in Burge Protestant Hospital, on July 15th. We named him Samuel. We now had two prophets to help all the kings we would meet, but it would be soon time to return to home. I called David to ask what he thought, and he replied that he felt that we should return home. We had learned to be submitted to authority, so we packed up and returned home.

BLOWN ABOUT BY THE WIND

It has been a marvelous experience. The wind bloweth where it listeth, and thou heareth the sound thereof, but canst not tell whence it cometh, and whither it goeth: so is everyone that is born of the spirit. These of course are the words of Jesus...John 3:8.

From the beginning of my Spiritual life, for the most part I have always felt that this verse best explained my life. It has always seemed that God just sovereignly moved in and out of my life as he chose.

I began without any knowledge of the Bible, yet I was being moved by an unseen, yet gentle force into the will and purpose of God. It was as if I was just a leaf being blown about in a gentle breeze. Time and time again the gifts, talents and callings of God, just seemed to appear or happen in an easy, but powerful way.

At first, I didn't know about the gifts of the Spirit, they just started to work in my life. I would feel urged to speak out words to the church or to a person, and they would come to pass or be true. I would feel lead to pray over someone and they would be healed.

Once in a very large Assembly of God church in Philadelphia, while working in a Jewish mission it happened. I had never interpreted a message in tongues before. During the service a woman toward the rear of the church began to bring a message in tongues. Her voice was very loud and strong. The church hushed, we bowed, our heads in reverence.

Then as she brought her message to a close, I felt a powerful force began to move within me. I felt as if there was someone within me standing up and breathing very hard. Then in a moment I was on my feet giving the interpretation of that message to the church. It was powerful and when it was over, I was tired.

In the beginning of operating any Gift of the Spirit it was like that, but then as time progressed the feelings got softer and softer. I came to see that as I would continue to respond I began to know or sense, more than need to feel, the Spirit being powerful within me.

The time would come when I would get much direction from dreams. This makes many people nervous, thinking about being, lead around by dreams. Yet in over 48 years there was only one dream that was not accurate or not come to pass. That one about Bill Britain was only the beginning.

THE REVIVAL

I can't remember how it started, but we began to branch out to other groups in a neighboring State. Pastor Ferrero met Pastor Bob Justice an Advent Christian Pastor, from that State.

I began going to a home meeting in another town in that same State. As a result, several family's moved and joined our church Pastor Bob Justice later became a co- Pastor by Pastor Ferrero's humility. Pastor Bob and His wife Carolyn were a great asset to our church.

Then there were those of us that had a calling to the ministry but were as under shepherds. We were seen, as having a calling, but not fully matured in our ministry. Soon that would include Phil Cannistraci, Vance Holden, myself and from time to time there would be others.

Phil and his wife Pauline; with Elmer and his wife Delcie would purchase houses in Coventry near us. Vance and his wife Donna, I believe came from New York State. Sometimes Elmer's brother would visit. As these came so also the preaching and teaching expanded.

There were regular members of the congregation that were being encouraged to operate their gifts and talents as well.

The meetings were exciting you never knew what would happen or when. You didn't want to miss a meeting for fear of missing what God would be doing. The Lord was building a Church just as it was recorded in the New Testament.

There was also skepticism and I could understand it somewhat. The church was a good mixture. A few college professors, a few factory workers, some very immature very enthusiastic young men like me, but still a good mix. The young and less educated had grabbed this very quickly, while the older and more educated were hesitant about getting involved.

They could watch the young like me and see that I changed jobs a lot yet wanted to be called a minister. They found fault with one brother who always went out with his wife to eat a lot in restaurants yet needed to borrow money from the church to pay his bills. Still all in all we need to realize that young people need to grow up and will if we both let them and help them; Love them and not judge them.

MINISTER/CARPENTER

Everet Barth did that for me. He was a contractor and one day he asked would I work for him. What he did for me was nothing short of amazing.

It must have been the will of God for me to learn carpentry, for it has been my mainstay all my life. He was a very soft yet serious brother in the Lord. All the remainder of my life I would be both minister and carpenter. Everet did much more for me than do a good job of teaching me to be a carpenter. He took a real interest in my character. In a very awesome way he became my father.

Today we would say "mentor", but he was so much more. He would buy me lunch and teach me good habits.

I remember him saying, George you are going to be a very powerful minister someday and so you will have to learn how to interact with people. He spent much time trying to teach me manners and being polite. He taught me the part of life that my mother should have taught me.

I have prayed many times that I would become the man of God, that these men hoped that I would become. That I would be as humble as those I followed and as powerful as those I have walked with through the years. That's still my prayer.

We can do it, the world needs to see it, the Word of God declares it. We must lay aside every weight that does besets us and run with patience the race that is set before us. Heb. 12:1. Lay aside the pain the suffering, forgive and let go; and you will enter, into the world of the Holy Spirit, the world of the supernatural.

In the Bible, we are taught not to keep a record of the pain. May I add then don't keep a record of the wonderful things that God has done through you, lest you be lifted-up with pride. I Corin. 13.

Just repent of your sins and receive Jesus Christ as your Lord. Believe in the blood that he shed for you sins and make Him your Savior. Get baptized "in the name of the Lord Jesus Christ", by emersion for the remission of your sins. Then seek to be baptized with the Holy Spirit, evidenced by speaking in other tongues. In I John 5:8. it says, "that there are three that bear record in the earth; the Spirit, and the water, and the blood and these three agree in one". A threefold cord.

I know that people use I Corin. 12 to say "not all speak in tongues", but Corin. Is talking about "the gifts of the Spirit" the book of Acts is talking about the "baptism in the Holy Ghost". That's apples and oranges.

At one point the church came to an impasse. We could not get those who did not believe in the gifts of the spirit operating in the church, to be comfortable with those of us who operated them. So, the Pastor set aside every Saturday morning for a prayer/study breakfast. We spent many months discussing the problem and made some progress, however the main issue was not resolved.

I have found that when men are sincere in their efforts for God, that he will find a way to help them if they will earnestly seek his help. We are told in the Word of God to strive for the mastery, to contend for the faith, to press towards the mark.

It seems that we always exert every avenue before we sincerely seek the Lords will or solution to our problems. Yes, we prayed every day to get God to help us, but when I got desperate, I got an answer. I had gotten frustrated with nothing really getting better. One evening I got serious and decided that I would stay up all night in prayer asking God, to help us resolve this impasse. This would turn out to be the second time a Divine visitation would happen in my life. Talk about a surprise.

VISITATION II

Around 3:00 a.m. in the morning God spoke to me. It was not an audible voice, but it was so loud in my spirit that I answered audibly. He said, "FRIENDS" and I said out loud "ENEMIES" and He said, "NO STRANGERS". I could not believe my ears. What a simple solution, who, would have thought that the problem was not theological. It was something I would never have thought of, on my own.

We had never gotten to know each other personally, except at church. We were really strangers as far as really knowing each other. When I shared this experience with David, he suggested that we start having church dinners more often, and that helped a lot.

We began to find out that we were all just people and really very much alike. We all had similar dreams for ourselves, our children and our church. We all just wanted to be sure that what was going on was of God.

ROBERT SADDLER

There were friends of Pastor David that from time to time came by for a visit. Robert Saddler was one I would never forget. He was a large black brother. I doubt that there had ever been a black person in that church. I had never known a black person. I had seen a few black kids in high school but had never interacted with any of them.

He was so kind and gentle. He was soft spoken and easy to be around. In one service I remember, before he preached, he walked around hugging people. I thought that this is going to be interesting. I remember him hugging a college professor and saying, "Lord this is a good brother".

There was a moment in his life years before when he was driving in a wooded area. He felt the Spirit tell him to stop at a roadside rest stop and get out his pump organ and worship the Lord, so he did.

Down in the woods, unbeknown to Robert was a preacher fishing with his son. As Robert played and worshiped, they heard him and came up out of the woods. As the boy toped the edge of the road, he yelled to his father "dad there's a bear playing an organ." The preacher had gotten discouraged and backslidden.

Here at the side of the road God had drawn the man back to Himself, because Robert had obeyed what he felt was the leading of the Holy Spirit. You need to Read the life story of Robert Saddler.

THEY SHALL CAST OUT DEMONS AND HEAL THE SICK

There is another incident that stands out to me. Sandy and I were eating dinner one evening when the phone rang. It was Delcia, Elmer's wife. "Who is you family doctor?" "We don't have a family doctor", I replied. What is wrong? Elmer has bent over and can't straighten back up. They lived at Pine Lake Shores at the time; I told her we would come right over, and I called Phil. He got there before I did, and he was already praying over Elmer.

None of us can remember exactly whether we were trying to cast out a spirit of infirmity or just praying for healing; so I joined right in. We danced around for several minutes, then Elmer screamed, "It's gone," and he straightened up. It was over, and he was fine. That Elmer was healed is all that matters

AND THEN THERE WAS TED

Ted was a fellow that seemed to be a square peg in a round hole. His life had been filled with pain and so he did not look at life as others did. He just didn't fit in with the others in the church.

When he was young, he was raised with a lot of violence; later he enlisted into the Navy. So, his life was very hard and without much love.

When our son Nathan got very sick with measles or chicken pox, nothing we could do helped. One afternoon Ted came over, he said that he felt God wanted him to pray for Nate. I didn't think anything would come of it, but he prayed and left.

The next morning, we were awakened by Nathan standing in his crib just shaking it for all he was worth. I learned not to judge others, because we can't see into their hearts. Ted is really a very caring brother in Christ; he and I are close friends to this day.

One Sunday Ted gave a testimony of how God could change a life, but it was my life he was talking about. He said that he was repairing an IBM machine at the Thread Co. that I had worked at the summer I was off from High School.

He asked them did they remember George Freeman. "Oh yes we remember him". Well he's a preacher now. "Oh no, not him" they replied. Yes he is in the ministry. "Oh that must be a different person". No insisted Ted" he is the same one, only Jesus has changed his life". It was an awesome testimony. But mom didn't get the point and stayed mad at Ted for a long time.

VIRGINIA

In 1969, my mom got sick and died. Her Pastor told us that she had given her heart to Jesus a short time before. She had never told us, but we had noticed a change in her behavior. The Lord is good, all the time.

With both dad and mom gone we decided to move. Sandy had always wanted to live in the Shenandoah Valley, so we found a small farm above the valley. We put the house up for sale and got a loan for the farm, but we still needed moving expense money to get there.

I got a call to enclose a porch and bid the work at $2,100. I told them that I would need $700. Down to move my family to Virginia. That if they would give me the money as a down payment on the job, I would move my family and return to do the work. Come on would you give a stranger $700.00 to work for you when he was moving out of state? But they did.

So, we moved just before school started and I flew back to finish the job. Sandy had to meet the movers, get the furniture arranged and get the kids enrolled in school, all by herself. She did a super job as always. Love you baby.

ALL ALONE

It was 1970, and for the first time we were really on our own. We missed the saints back in the DePot, we were not near Sandy's folks, and we were alone. This was the start of a new chapter in the life of those that would grow up in Jesus Christ.

Standing in the shadows you'll find Jesus. Alone yet never alone.

The farm had 60 acres of land and a large barn. The house was two story with three large rooms on each floor. I closed in the rear porch for a laundry room, build a vanity in the bathroom and a counter that divided the kitchen to provide a dining area. Now we could settle down to living.

The interesting thing that we would find was, not being able to find, a spiritual Church in our area. The churches were nice family things, but not moving in the Spirit, like we were used to. As we kept looking for a home church, we finely found one that seemed to be in the Spirit, about 10 miles away.

I was able to find employment with a Baptist preacher who was also a contractor. I worked for him till I could find better paying work in a large city, near- by. That work was building a very exclusive housing development. While there I met another carpenter that was ministering to some college kids in a big city.

COLLEGE KIDS & THE DREAM

While working with the brother in the housing development, he invited me to come to the home meetings he was having with college kids, on Thursday evenings.

One night after I had been going for several weeks, I had a dream. In the dream he was in my front yard. He put his bare foot up on the chopping block and raised the ax. He was going to cut his foot and I yelled to him, stop. In the dream I said, "don't cut your toes off you will lose your balance," then I was awake. I knew that if you saw someone about to cut his foot, you would say don't hurt yourself. You wouldn't say anything about balance. I gathered from that, that the man was doing something that was unbalancing his ministry to those college kids.

The next Thursday I took him into the kitchen privately and told him the dream. I expected him to say that he didn't understand it. So, I was very surprised when he said, "I know what that is about." I was taken back by his humility.

He explained that he and his wife were on the outs and he was living in that house with some of the college girls. He admitted that he was being tempted by them. So, we prayed that God would work that out and I left.

The following Thursday, before the meeting he took me into the kitchen and told me. "The next day, on the strength of that dream he called his wife and they worked out their differences". He moved back home that same day. Praise the Lord for the man's humility and the Lords help.

We went on to have many good times with those kids. Some of them gave their lives to the Lord. Some of them got baptized in the Holy Spirit. There were a few healings and one very interesting experiment.

At one meeting the students told me that one of the girl's mother, had forbidden her to come to any more of the meetings. They asked, "Should we tell her to sneak out." My answer surprised them.

I told them to tell the girl, to do everything her mother asks her to do. To keep up her homework, to keep her room clean and to ask her mother if there were any chores she could do. They acted as if that was crazy, but they said that they would tell her.

In a few weeks the girl is back, and her mother came with her. She wanted to see who made such a change in her daughter's attitude. Most parents just want to see what, their kids are into.

CHURCH

We were looking for a good church, so we went to a small white church near our farm and they welcomed us warmly. They had no Pastor except each Sunday a different minister would speak. They didn't have any mid-week services, just Sunday morning. We checked out the other church's we could find, but they all seemed more like nice friendly clubs, rather than churches. Everybody it seemed went to church, but they all tended to be, more religious, than spiritual. It was just a nice friendly religious neighborhood.

I don't remember how we met Ruth Williams, but she was going to a Pentecostal church about 10 miles away.

We decided to try it and were pleasantly surprised. The church was into the moving of the Holy Spirit, and they wanted to follow Jesus. We fit right in and really enjoyed ourselves. After a few months Pastor Woods asked me to preach some. They had Sandy sing often as well.

In the fullness of time he asked me to teach the adult Sunday school class, which I did until the Woods left to take another church. For a few years we kept in touch with them.

I kept going to the Thursday night meetings until we started a job in North Carolina. The carpenter that held the meetings with the college kids knew a man in North Carolina that wanted to build a sub-division of 50 homes. We would need to live there to do that. So, he provided us a farmhouse there to use each week. We agreed to work four, ten- hour days to get a three, day weekend; that made our wives very happy.

We had a problem of fixing meals before and after work because we were tired. So, we wondered if one of our wives would come down for the entire week to fix breakfast and supper. They all agreed, so each week a different wife would room with her husband and cook that week.

On the week Sandy came she bought Nate and Sam with her. We all had a good time that week. At some point we caught three baby Raccoons, and I built a chicken wire cage to keep them in. We played with them and fed them with, kids' baby bottles.

Once the three houses were finished the owner decided not to do any more. Every night after work we taught the young men from the Bible. We had a great time in God's Word. I missed that when we, had to go back home.

THE FIRE

Sandy began to miss her family and started thinking about us moving to West Virginia, onto her father's farm.

About that time, we had a house fire. Our mischievous son Samuel was out on the back porch playing. We had a gas dryer that had stopped working. I had turned off the gas and ordered a part for the dryer. While Sam played there, he put his hand under the dryer and turned the gas valve. Out came the gas and a spark ignited the gas. The fire started, and the kids were trapped there. Sandy tried to get to them, but the flames were too high, so she told them to go jump into the pond.

She calmly called the fire department. The fire department put out the fire, and the ambulance took all three to the hospital in Roanoke.

I was at work, and after work I called home to see if Sandy needed anything. A neighbor woman answered the phone. As I wondered, why is she answering; she told me that I needed to get home. When I arrived home, there was smoke everywhere and several fire trucks in the front yard. The fire chief told me that the fire was out, and my family was in an ambulance on the way to the city.

In the hospital, I found out that all three of them were burned. Sandy had burned her legs trying to get to the kids. Nathan was burned over his face and body, but he was, burned the least. Sam was badly burned on his body, but his arm was burned worst of all. Nathan's body healed the fastest of the three. Sandy was not able to walk for some time, but she healed completely. Sam would carry a scar on his upper right arm for most of his life, he was the last to leave the hospital.

We have much to praise God for as we are all alive and well. This helped us to decide to move. We sold the house and on April first, 1974, we made ready to move.

We got the longest overhead moving van we could rent because we had two cars, plus the moving van to get to West Virginia. We put the small boxes up over the cab and then I drove our Renault into the van. We placed pillows and bedding into the car, and garden tools under it; works for me. Then the heavy furniture and beds. I drove the van and Sandy drove our other car.

WEST VIRGINIA HERE TO STAY

In West Virginia, as we unloaded the van her little cousin Richie yelled "there's a car in the van" and we all laughed. We finally got unloaded and settled in. That was a very busy and tiring weekend.

In the days ahead, I went looking for a house for us to rent, and a job for me. I think that the employment came first, and then we found some people moving out of a large house nearby.

I had gotten a job working, building a large sub-division up above the town. They built 28 homes, I was over 14 and another man was over the other 14.

We moved to West Virginia the first weekend in April and moved into this nice four, bedroom house in mid-August, in time to register the boys in school. We stayed there for about 15 years.

With the kids in school, and me working, everything settled down. At one place the homeowners were selling their old kitchen cabinets, with all the appliances. Our kitchen only had an old metal cabinet. I told the landlord that if he would pay for the new stuff, I would install it. He gave me the $200 dollars and in three days I had put it all in.

The cabinets were beautiful, all the appliances came with it. Everything fit perfectly. Sandy was in her glory. It's good to make your wife happy.

The house had a full basement with a coal furnace, a large dining room and a full width front living room. Upstairs there were four bedrooms, and a full attic. It was just perfect for us. There was a large rear yard and an extra lot for a garden.

I was able to heat the house with 10 ton of coal that cost $250.00 Dollars per winter. I had to shovel the coal into the bin and then into the furnace. Once a week I had to shovel the ashes into a bucket and dump them in a ravine next to the house. I really enjoyed living there.

THE FIRST SONG

One day as I shoveled coal into the furnace the Spirit put a song in my heart. "Turn it on and let it burn, till it burns away my dross. Till my heart is all aflame seeing Jesus on the cross". I have always been amazed at how and what God can do in your life when you let him be Lord.

THE HOLY FIRE OF GOD

TURN IT ON AND LET IT BURN. TILL IT BURNS WITHIN MY SOUL:

TILL THE HOLY FIRE OF GOD CLEANSES ME AND MAKES ME WHOLE.

TURN IT ON AND LET IT BURN, TILL IT BURNS AWAY MY DROSS:

TILL MY HEART IS ALL AFLAME, SEEING JESUS ON THE CROSS.

SO, TURN IT ON AND LET IT BURN,

TILL MY LIFE IS ALL CONSUMED: TILL THE HOLY FIRE OF GOD, HAS MY SACRIFICE APPROVED.

Given in 1975 to G.B.F.

THE CHURCH

Somehow when I was doing remodeling, I met a family that was going to Pastor Mark Adam's church. She was very excited about it and invited us to come, so we did. We really fell in love with what was going on there. It was the liveliest and friendliest church that we had ever been to since leaving my home state.

The Holy Spirit was moving all the time. The worship and Praise was fantastic, and the gifts of the Spirit were in great operation. What surprised me the most was that the doctrine was in total harmony with mine. That has never been a major issue with me, but it was a nice fit, it just seemed that everything was in place.

It was obvious that God was being allowed to build his church the way He wanted to do it. The building was a beautiful small old church building in a nearby city. The parking would become the problem in time. It got to be that, every week new families and singles were coming to see for themselves what was going on there. In less than a year we removed the pews and put in chairs. The chairs made room for extra seating. The people kept pouring in, and before we left, there were people sitting on the platform.

The building was maxed out and the parking lot was maxed out, so we decided to raise money to move. They had started a Christian day school. It had become obvious to Christians everywhere that the, public school system was going atheistic and teaching evolution, sex Ed. and a host of non-Christian ideals.

THE MIRACLE

We left and found a small church below Shinnston. They were a country type and had a very relaxed atmosphere. The pastor was old, but a very spirited fellow. In time they found a nicer church building and decided to move there, but I felt to stay and Pastor this one.

Nathan finally started playing the piano and God began to move. A young woman that was backslidden started coming and came back to the Lord. We asked her to lead worship and she did a real fine job. Her father was a backslidden preacher and soon he started coming.

He was a good man, but some of his people had discouraged him from preaching. After a time, his other daughter started coming also. We were building a crowd; things were moving along well.

The preachers, wife had been diagnosed with a bad heart condition and was on seven kinds of medication. One day I got a phone call from our worship leader the women's daughter. She asked if I would come and pray for her mother, I said sure.

When I arrived, I got the surprise of my life. On every kitchen cabinet door there was a large sheet of paper taped to the door with a healing scripture verse on each one. She told me that, for the last several weeks she had come over and had her mother read every verse out loud. I believe that she did that twice each day.

Then she addressed me saying "Now if you will pray the prayer of faith my mother will be healed". I thought to myself sister you have the faith. So, we agreed in prayer, praised the Lord for the answer and I went home. At her mothers, next Doctors appointment he pronounced her healed and took her off all her medication. Now, she started to come to church also.

Sandy was teaching the children and Nathan was playing the piano. There were several teenagers coming, it seemed that the Lord was doing us good. We were there for several years when a minister I had never heard of called me.

PRIDE GOETH BEFORE A FALL

His name was Ben; He said that he had heard of me and wanted to talk with me, so we got together and talked. He told me that he was sent here by prophetic word and was building a large church. That he wanted me to join him in building a great work for God. "That sounded good to me", so I talked to my members and we closed our church and merged with Ben and I became one of his elders. We were meeting in a nice building in the country. Here again the Spirit was moving and there were four or five gifts of the Spirit operating in every meeting. I was prophesying in many of the services.

One night I had a dream. In the dream we were having a funeral service for one of the older elders Bro. Mack Jones. In the dream I was up in the rafters looking down and watched them wheel in the casket up the center isle and set it in front of the pulpit. When, they opened the casket it was Bro. Jones. Later that morning I called Pastor and asked him if Bro. Jones was sick. He said that he hadn't heard of that and did not believe that he was. About 30 days later we did Bro. Jones's funeral, just as I had seen it in the dream.

Soon people began coming, soon the church was really growing. Eventually there were over 200 people in the congregation. It was flat out and moving, it was great. If you wanted a front seat you had to go a half an hour early. Usually there were 25-30 young people at the altar praying before every service. There were healings, miracles, tongues and prophecy's all the time.

THE PROPHET COVERED MY SHOULDER

I don't remember the time frame, but a prophet trained under A.A. Allen came to the city; to the Armory, his last name was Duncan. Sandy and I were seated on aisle seats about 1/2 of the way back. I dressed in casual clothes so as not to suggest that I was in ministry.

During one of his services he started down the aisle shaking hands while he was preaching. He took my hand as he was walking by but didn't let go. He stopped and asked me to stand up. "Would you mind if I do something different?" he asked. I answered no so he took off his jacket and put it over my shoulders and prophesied that God had called me to be a prophet like himself. He took his jacket and moved on.

This Was a conformation to us, as we had been in the ministry for more than 20 years at that time. It is always good to have God still speaking into your life.

THE GHOST WHO WALKS

Somewhere in the mid-eighties, Sandy and I resigned from that church and began to wait on the Lord for direction.

We had been praying for about three months when one day I heard a horn blowing in the driveway. It was a good friend of ours, Pastor Jack Bissett. He said, "I have been meaning to tell you of a church up near Wallace", so I hopped in the car and off we went.

We met Okie Jones. That had been his church in days gone by. He and his wife were very old and sick. They had let many people try to start the church up again, but it never lasted more than a few months.

I asked him for the key. I told him I would like to keep the key for a few weeks so that my wife and I could pray in the building, to see how we felt about it. He agreed, and we left for home. Later people asked, "How did you get a key?" Okie wouldn't give out keys to anyone.

I called the building, the ghost who walks, it looked like it had been dead for 50 years. It had not been painted or cared for in that long of a time.

The windows had been painted over, there was no water and the electric, and was only 110 V. Even the pews were first generation, homemade. What was the worst, was that the basement wall was falling in. What's not to like! What?

What we didn't know was that while we were in the building a hurricane went through the area. It rained very hard and I found only one leak in the roof, that's nice. When we left for home there were branches everywhere.

When we finished praying, I was in the rear of the sanctuary, and Sandy was at the altar. She rose to her feet and came toward me and as she turned toward me, a thought started in my head. "If this was on Main Street, we would take it". As this ran through my head, she opened her mouth and said, "if this was on main street, we would take it," and I got mad. What is all this about?

We closed the door, got into the car, and started driving toward home and she asked me, "What are you mad about"? What could I be mad about? "This is way out in the country, nobody will come." Look at all the work that needs to be done. "I am better than this". I should have a church on Main Street. God "had nailed me to the floor." I never thought I was being pride full! What I am glad for is; that I humbled myself and that we decided to open the church.

It was spring, and I called everyone I knew that was, backslidden or not going to church anywhere. I had asked the Lord for a sign. I planned to ask for an offering to work on the building. I asked the Lord for at least $100 dollars. There was about 25 people that sat in our living room. I told them the story and asked how many would start the church with us. To a person they all agreed. Then I asked an offering, I held my breath, it was over $300 dollars. Praise be to the Lord.

The building needed a lot of work and until some of it got done, I was afraid to let anyone, see it. Sandy and I cleaned and scraped the windows, walls and floors.

We set up chairs in the back yard and had meetings every Sunday, as it was summer. In the, mean time I asked Willie, Tom and another brother to help me repair the basement wall.

When we met at the church for the first time, I gave Willie a key to the church. He cried and said that no one had ever given him a key to a church before. I believed that was because he was black.

Tom looked me in the eye and asked, are you telling me that God told you to take this church? I answered yes, and He said that if I could not have said yes, that he was not going to go with us.

A SMALL MIRACLE

The block foundation had broken along the entire side and was bowing in at least 4". We would need to remove the dirt away from the building all the way down to the footer.

I knew that I needed to brace the wall on the inside to keep the wall stable while we dug. I was totally surprised to find that it only took us three days to do all that digging.

We were finished about 3pm the last afternoon and I didn't know what else to do, so I sent them home. I just went down into the basement to pray. As I prayed, I walked along on the braces, that's when it happened.

As I stepped from one brace to another, I noticed the next brace slide down a little. Thrilled, I was ecstatic, I knew at once what was happening, the wall was going back into place.

Within an hour of walking on the braces the wall was back into perfect condition, all we would need to do was B-bond both sides. I went home and called willie, he was mad "why didn't you let us stay and see the miracle?", I wish I had. I could never have envisioned this. It's true "God is able to do exceedingly abundantly above all that you can ask or think." We've got His word on it. Eph. 3:20.

In September, I believe; the Lord spoke to me to open the church the first Sunday in October, the 4th. The work was almost finished, the city water had been connected, we had cleaned up the property and made a sign. The sign was made on a sheet of plywood between two 4x4's across the road at the end of the parking lot. The only, thing left, was to get the furnace running.

No sweat, Willie and Tom worked for the gas company. The Man from the gas company came out and turned the meter on. We went into the building and could smell gas but could not find any leaks. He said that the leaks must be outside, and he would need to turn off the meter and lock it. I asked him would he leave it unlocked and gave him my word as a Pastor that we would not turn it on until we had repaired the lines and the leaks. He agreed and left.

THREE SMALL MIRACLES

Friday, we returned with what we needed and found that the line was under the road, which we could not dig up. To our amazement we found that the original line had been put through an old drain culvert, so we just pushed and pulled the new one through and connected it to the meter. One small miracle. Saturday morning, October 3rd we return.

We plan to replace the iron line. As we dug along the foundation, we found that the black iron pipe that fed the gas to the church had rusted full of pin holes. It is noon time, where can we get a joint of pipe here in this wilderness? We are 2.5 hours round trip to a big city, so we go 15 minutes to the next small town, and there in the wilderness is a fully stocked hardware store. We get everything we need and back at the building we finish the repairs. It is 4pm and we turn on the gas, no leaks, we shout for joy. The second miracle. But the furnace won't ignite. Tom says, "I thought you were moving too fast". I don't know what to do, so we go home.

On the way home, I prayed and asked the Lord what to do, He gave me a man's name. I called him as soon as I got home, and he told me to take the orifice apart and blow it out.

I hopped into the car and drove back to the church it is only 45 minutes away. I did what he said, and the furnace fired up. A third miracle. Four small miracles and a lot of hard work and Sunday morning October 4th the Sun is shining bright, but not as bright as the SON. Praise be to the lord. He got it done.

The first service was wonderful, but small. I had trusted a family that I thought could handle the shabby looking building, but it was more than they could believe for. They came back and said, "We are not going with you, Bro. Freeman, you have bitten off more than you can chew." He then told others, so that first Sunday, there were only about 8 or 10 of us there to enjoy the blessings of the Lord.

As time went on, we painted the building, upgraded the power to 220 v., added new lights and partitioned the basement for classrooms. A good number of folks in the area were coming and many of the original people came too.

Sandy became the piano player and some of the ladies started doing specials. Tom and his wife Kathleen took over the children's class, and Willie took the teenagers. It was really purring now.

One Sunday Jack and his wife came. We welcomed them with open arms. I asked him to preach and he did a good job. We were running about 35-40 and the interesting thing was that the attendance was the same all three services. It was a very lively congregation and a very happy one.

There was a man who had three teens, and they came every week. I went down to see them and he told me, my girls really like going there. I was just amazed because we really didn't seem to have much to interest them. The Spirit of the Lord was very marvelous.

A VERY SPECIAL GUEST

One time we had Dan Waldheim, from Maryland, come and preach a revival. In one service he called four people up front to speak what he felt was the "Word of the Lord" over them. He called them from different sections of the sanctuary, but they were all members of one family. Each word was right on, it was awesome.

SOME VERY SPECIAL MEN

I was blessed to have some young men that worked with me. I had the privilege of helping them with their training. There was Willie, Ron Lee, Bee Gee, Tom, and Jack. When the time came for us to go our separate ways most of them would go on to their own ministry.

I have always believed in body ministry and an open pulpit. I have told many people, of the days at Dola. I said," we had 6,or 8 preachers and they all knew from the start that they could preach anytime they felt lead, but there were no claw marks on the pulpit."

A very special blessing, a lovely young lady named Stacie came there and when our son Nathan wasn't playing the piano, he started sitting next to her.

THE RESULTS

Jack and his wife felt to go on to join another organization, they trained for a year and were given a nice church. I questioned it but later realized that they fit like a hand in a glove. It was perfect. He had me come do revivals for him. Some came to Jesus, some rededicated their lives, at least one got called into the ministry. He died suddenly, and they had the largest funeral I have ever seen about 500 people.

Ron Lee was an Evangelist, one of the best I have ever known. You will long remember the messages Ron preaches. I still remember "You are knocking on the wrong door". He went on to Pastor several churches and has had me preach in them.

Willie and Be Ge have gone on to have long time ministries in the area; they are great servants of the Lord, and to this day, no sacrifice is too much for them.

Jeff came back to the Lord in one of these meetings and has a great ministry pastoring in a large church in a nearby city.

YOUR GIFT

"A man's gift makes room for him". A very powerful scripture and one we should heed. Prov. 18:16. God gives the gift, we do not get to pick our own. "He gives severally as it pleases Him". What we need to do is to accept each man's gift and reverence it. I Corin. 12-14.

A very wonderful brother I know, was a very gifted Evangelist and saw many people saved and filled with the Holy Spirit. A man who owned a store told him that he should Pastor and so he started in that direction.

He worked with a large church until He got badly hurt and left the ministry for a long time. He finally came back, but he was afraid to trust anyone and became prideful and has since fallen away. Let us be careful how we deal with each other.

In the late 80's we lost the use of the building and merged with another ministry. I told the Pastor that I just wanted to keep them together until I could find another building. I wasn't wanting to preach, just to be there. He made us feel right at home. We all got along wonderfully. It is good when brethren get along together in unity. All winter we worshiped and preached together. It was great, the singing, and the preaching it all was great.

It was such a joy to see us all flowing together in the work of the Lord. One of the brothers got up one meeting and said that he felt to go to Florida and work there. Immediately I felt that the Spirit said to me. "Tell him I did not tell him to go. Tell him not to go and if he go's he will suffer hurt." He was at the front, so I walked up to him and prophesied to him not to go, but he went and several months later, He returned with only his truck and personal possessions, he had lost everything.

The devil hates it when brothers walk together in harmony and in the Spirit. When summer arrived, one by one the ministers left. Finally, there was just Sandy and I besides the Pastor.

The events of this year had, worn me out, so I thought I am going to take a break. All this time I was employed by the county. So, for a few years I just worked my job and went to someone else's church.

OUR KIDS

The kids had graduated from High school and were in college. They were having the time of their lives with school and basketball. Sam had tried his hand at dating, and I believe Nate took a girl out a few times. When moms do a good job of loving their sons the boys don't feel the need for girls as much as boys not gentled by moms.

The truth is I threatened to "padlock the fridge". Really, I have always felt that we had the best two boys in the world.

THE BOYS

We have two lively sons. Nathan is one year and four days older than Samuel. They have very similar features, but very different personalities.

Nathan even at a young age manifested a selflessness that is amazing. He is soft, quiet, easy going, like his mother. Samuel is energetic, adventurous; he likes to get into things, like his father.

They both like sports and choose basketball as their school sport. They grew up in church's that for the most part, are, lead, of the Holy Spirit. They are shown good Christian lifestyles by family and church members.

In the boy's early school years, the teachers and subjects had a good moral undertone, but that has changed as the years moved by. The need for Bible based teaching in schools is now obvious. With the teaching having become atheistic, the morals of our youth and adults have fallen drastically in the last 40 years.

The school is now 12 hours a day with after school sports, and games on Sundays, the atheist's church. The price is evident even physically, with almost 2 million high school youth; with broken bones, brain damage, or dead as a results of high school sports. It's time to end the carnage.

Nate, and Sam played ball so well that no one would let them both play on the same team, because they could not be beaten. Sam went on to play ball in High school and today 35 years later he still holds 5 records.

Is life all sports, are there not girls? And what of Stacie?

NATHAN AND STACIE

During the summer of 1988 an event happened that would change and shape the course of my life. My dad was pastoring a church in Dola, West Virginia, and his church had a swimming pool party at the public pool in Shinnston, West Virginia. I left work and drove to the Shinnston swimming pool to attend the party.

A woman named Ethel, who attended my father's church, had invited her niece Stacie Danielle to the pool party. That evening I met Stacie for the first time in my life. She was a beautiful young woman.

Several weeks went by and my dad's church had a weekend revival during the weekend of Labor Day in September 1988. I played the piano for the worship service at the revival services.

After one of the church services was over, while I was still sitting at the piano bench, Stacie walked up to the piano and told me that her phone number was in the book. I called her that week and arranged to go out on our first date that next weekend.

Before I picked her up for our first date, she told me that her parents wanted to meet me. At the time Stacie was 17 years old (about four months from her 18th birthday) and I was 25. Her dad showed me the gun room in the house, it had lots of guns.

Our first date was at the Western Steer steak house in Fairmont. Stacie was shy and did not like to eat in front of me. She did not eat very much of her food at the restaurant on our first date and I joked with her, that she could box up her food and send it to the children in Africa or something like that.

Stacie became a Christian at the age of eight years old and grew up in a Baptist church in West Virginia. As we were dating, she started going to church with me. She was not used to being in Pentecostal or charismatic church's but continued to attend church services with me and had an interest in spiritual things and the things of God. We had many exciting and fun adventures and good times during our dating relationship.

During part of our engagement period I had moved to San Diego, California, to accept employment with Morris Cerrullo ministry. Since these were the days before cell phones, we talked on the phone probably about every day, sometimes maybe multiple times a day, and sometimes for long periods of time.

When I came back from San Diego, California, we got married and Stacie had a phone bill from her parents that was about 27 pages long and I believe totaled over $600 dollars.

I moved back to West Virginia from California in November of 1991 and we were getting married the next month. I had not had a haircut in a long time and literally the day I moved back was the same day that Stacie was having her wedding shower. That was the first time that Stacie had seen me in several weeks and she thought I looked like I had stepped out of the 1960s with my long hair.

We were married at Calvary Temple. We had been attending that church right before I moved to California.

The Pastor there, and my dad both performed parts of the wedding ceremony between Stacie and myself. It was a beautiful wedding ceremony with a very large wedding party. All together I think we had about 18 people in our wedding party. Several of my very closest friends were my groomsmen and my brother, Samuel Freeman, was my best man in the wedding.

Approximately one year later, on December 30, 1992 we welcomed our first child into the world. His name means anointed or appointed one. Then about five, and one-half years later, on June 8, 1998, our second child named Caleb Bruce Freeman was born and we celebrated his arrival into our family. Caleb's name means bold one.

Our sons both attended Heritage Christian School for many years. We also home schooled each of our sons for part of their education. Our first son graduated from High School in 2011. Caleb graduated from Heritage Christian School in 2016.

One of the things that I have learned from several years of marriage is that you need to honor your wife and put her first in the relationship after God. Your wife must feel loved and very important to her husband and that she is special to him.

Also, when you have an argument with your wife don't let the sun go down on your wrath. Discuss issues and talk things out before you go to sleep. Don't let problems and arguments fester for long periods of time but work to resolve issues with you and your spouse.

Finally, one of the most important things in a marriage is to not give up but determine in your mind and heart that you are in this relationship for the long haul. Divorce should not be an option. Be willing to roll up your sleeves and make a lasting commitment to your marriage partner.

Our oldest son married a lovely young girl that he had met in college. They lived with us for about the first 15 months of their marriage. They have a beautiful baby boy. We enjoy spending time with our family.

We just celebrated our 27th wedding anniversary on December 28, 2018. I have been truly blessed with a wonderful and beautiful wife. Stacie is a wonderful wife and a great Christian woman, and awesome mother. She loves the Lord and loves being involved in church, in kid's ministry and in vacation Bible school.

We have been blessed with our son and our wonderful daughter-in-law and beautiful grandsons.

They both really love the Lord and have been two of the finest sons any father and mother could ask for. Stacie and I are both very proud of our two young men and love them very much.

We are not perfect but when you try to stay in church and love the Lord and center your life on Jesus, great things happen. We are thankful for each other and our Christian sons and Christian home.

SAMUEL AND CHERYL

Sam Freeman met Cheryl Steffich at Faith Fellowship Church in 1991. They were set up for a date by a widow in the church who must have seen the potential.

They dated for 2 years, then got engaged and waited 2 more years until Cheryl finished Pharmacy School at WVU.

They married in 1995 and moved to Waldorf, MD in the Washington, DC area. Cheryl was the Children's Church Director in Maryland. Sam became an ordained minister and was the Worship Leader.

They have 2 wonderful children, Courtney Grace & Joshua Luke. Courtney is a sophomore at WVU and Josh is a Junior at Bridgeport High School. They both have been involved in sports, youth group, music, and have received academic awards. They have been in church all their lives and it shows.

The whole family has proven themselves of the highest caliber and as having an unvarnished passion to serve others in the Lord. They all are in some form of ministry for the Lord Jesus

Both of our sons have been born again and been filled with the Holy Spirit. To have experienced Jesus Christ and been raised in a Christian environment does mean everything in building a successful life.

Nate liked to play the piano and sing. Sam would sing along with him sometimes. Today they are both in worship ministries in their respective churches. They have grown up into two of the most respected men in this area. They are known for their honesty, integrity, and their family mindedness. They put their family's needs before their own. Their Biblical knowledge coupled with common sense wisdom is known to all.

The results are obvious, the four grandchildren are also born again and most of them are filled with the Holy Spirit. They are all in some form of ministry serving the Lord as their parents do. Sandy made that possible. She is the most serious and spiritual wife and mother we could have ever had, She's just plainly and simply the best.

ANOTHER OLD COUNTRY CHURCH

Every once and awhile Pastor David Kates, would drop in at the office and tell me that there was a vacant church on an old country rd. He said, "You need to look at it." I would say thanks, some time I will. This happened at least three times that year and so one day I drove by.

Boy that is a nice building, I like that, I wonder why it is vacant. Sandy and I looked at the building and talked with the owner. She decided to rent it to us, so we started in the early-mid 90's. This would be the first church that had a church office in it; that I could use for my books and as a study.

We started with about thirty folks, half of us white folks and half of us anointed folks. Some of them were the remnants of Dola.

When I realized a fellow that I had been witnessing to for years lived just up the hill I started talking to him. He just said keep praying for me, so I did. I kept asking God to show me what to say to him that would, get him back in church.

Then I thought, I'll pack my books and have Cleve help me carry them into the church. When we had done that, I said Cleve one of these pews has your name on it. He said that's nice and I took him home. So much for the ideas of men.

I kept praying and one day I felt that God gave me a thought. So, near the end of the week I went to his house and told him, Cleve it won't get easer, to come to church next month or next year. Saturday night go into the bathroom and look, at yourself in the mirror, eyeball to eyeball, and say, old boy tomorrow morning you are going to get up and go down to the church.

Believe it or not, Sunday he showed up and not only that, he kept coming every week thereafter. He had been out of church for more than 10 years, and now he was back to stay. Cleve has a heart of gold. He has so much compassion, he is like a big old teddy bear. He is rock solid in his lifestyle and in his teaching.

Years later he now has a prison ministry in three prisons. It is awesome. Cleve became my assistant pastor and we combed the countryside leaving tracts and praying for people. We just kept preaching, praying, and working.

Up the hill by the church lived a family that the Lord really got a hold on. They drove into the parking lot once but couldn't get their nerve up to come in. They seemed excited when we visited them but would not come down, so I set to praying for them.

After many weeks the Lord showed me to go to her house and pray over them. We prayed, and I left, the next Sunday she showed up. She came most of the time that we were there, Praise be to the Lord.

ANOTHER MIRACLE

We had about 10-15 rowdy teenagers, but not a good way to bring them. We also had three different shades of red carpet in the sanctuary. We were trying to raise $300 dollars for a set of videos for the teens, without much progress. So, we wanted a van, some carpet and those videos.

Then I got the phone call. Pastor Freeman can you bring me to church. Sure Judy, where do you live. She told me, and we started picking her up for church.

Years ago, back at Dola, Sandy had had a dream that Susan was going to give us a lot of money for the church, but that never happened. Judy had been a biker mom, so it is nice to have her in church. She is also Susan's daughter.

As we try to raise the funds to buy the videos Judy writes us a check for the$300 dollars. She has never worked, so I call the bank before I deposit the check, and am told its o.k. We get the video for the teens.

A few weeks later she says to me. "Pastor, next week I'm going to write you a check that's going to knock your socks off." I say thanks, and tell Sandy, she may give us a check for a thousand dollars. Sunday, after church she asks, "how do you want the check written out" I tell her to "Jesus is lord Tabernacle".

When I get the check it's for $10,000 dollars, written to George Freeman. I thank her and call the bank, understand this woman has never worked in her life and has no income. The bank says "you will have no problem with that check, I am floored, but I deposit the check. Oh yes, in the church's account. Praise be to the Lord!

I talked to the land lady about the color of the carpet and she agreed. Cleve and I put down light purple on the platform, the main floor, and in the overflow sanctuary, with $5,000 dollars of that money. It looked gorgeous. Everyone raved about it, except the land lady. You picked it I told her, you picked it.

THE VAN

I went looking for a passenger, van. That was hard to find. I covered all the car dealers for a used van, either the price was way above what we could handle, or they just did not have one. I was getting discouraged; then I drove into an auto dealer in Clarksburg. There's was a beauty, clean, white and a 15 passenger, but the price was $7,000 dollars. Well here goes nothing. I sit down and tell him who I am, and as a Pastor I have 15 teenagers to transport from Ratclif to our church. I started to explain the tragedy of them living in that place, but he cuts me off. "Let me make a phone call". He calls another dealer and asks if he can sell the van to me. The man agrees. He turns to me and says I know that area, I will sell you that van for $5,000 dollars.

The compassion of that man, even, the remembrance of it brings me to tears, 24years later. He knew the poverty, the open sewers. The burnt-out homes. Three of these teen age girls had one mother, but different fathers, and the man in the house now was not their father. You don't want to know the story you don't want to know their pain. They all seemed crazy, crazy for a reason.

One of the teenage boys seemed wild. His parents didn't want him and had given him to his grandfather to raise. He took him and did the best he could, but he was an alcoholic. The boy is raised in that environment and has no compass. He's adrift in a sea he can't control, of course he's crazy, you would be too. Train up a child…Prov. 22:6.

Everything that we were able to do for those teens was made possible with the money Judy had given us.

Would you like to hear the rest of the story? Remember the dream Sandy had about Susan giving the church a lot of money, well she did, in a way. After we left Dola, Susan was killed in a car accident. In time the other driver was found at fault and his insurance had to pay Judy $100,000 dollars. Judy had called another church for a ride to their church which was closer to her house. They couldn't be bothered, so she called us. They would have gotten the tithe, if they had just gone out of their way for a troubled young woman.

CLARENCE WILDER

Nathan and Stacie came from their church to help us, Nathan led the Worship and Praise. It was awesome we really had great services. The presence of the Lord was wonderful. Stacie did a marvelous job with the teens she was really wonderful.

I called Clarence, and we had him hold revivals three times. He came from across the river I believe. He was marvelous, He was exciting, and the altar services were out of sight. People were being healed all over the place. Many were falling out or being slain in the Spirit.

A real good friend of mine Pastor Roberts and his wife came to some of these services. His wife had hurt her neck in an accident, years before, and was in almost constant neck pain. When Evangelist Wilder prayed over her, she was instantly healed and suffers no pain still today.

Sandy stood by my side all through this ministry. Here as at Dola, she played the piano some, taught the youth, cleaned and cooked. She and Stacie worked hard and tirelessly at everything they did.

There is no way we could have had church without them and all the others that made the church what it became, especially Ron, Willie, and Be Ge. Like as at Dola, we pulled together and made it work.

There was a young Pastor and his wife that had a church in the country. One time I preached there for them. I felt to preach something about the cost of disobedience. I might have shared about a preacher who kept flying around looking at church designs for him to copy. One time his wife said for him to stop that and just work on his own church. Soon after a friend called, and they flew up to look at another church. They crashed in a storm and died, the price of disobedience.

After the service the Pastor and his wife brought their son up for prayer. He had wanted to go somewhere in his car, but they forbid him. He got mad and raced off in the car and crashed it into a tree. He was not hurt, but they felt that he had given into a spirit of rebellion. We prayed for his deliverance.

Once a month we had a worship service on Friday night. We invited anyone to come sing and play, and worship together. They were awesome, there is so much talent in the body of Christ. It was at one of these that Pastor Willy and I met, but there is one more story to tell.

THE OLD RED HEAD

Bob and Georgianna had wanted to come to church with us, but she had been in the hospital for three months. She kept calling to tell us that they were coming, they just hadn't shown up yet.

I had an old red head friend from Belpre, Ohio. He came to a local church two or three times a year; his name was Jerry Cochran.

Jerry, was the easiest man to be around. Always relaxed, always friendly just seemed happy all the time. He had a good evangelistic ministry. I don't believe he could read, he carried his Bible, but he always had someone read his text. I do believe that he must have studied tapes, because he quoted a lot of Scriptures.

He was preaching at the Pastors church that weekend and, I called him. He said that he was leaving Sunday morning for home. I asked would he preach for me that morning and he agreed. So, he followed us to the church; and we began the service.

We had great worship and singing and just as we were ending that part of the service, I noticed Bob and Georgianna come in. We sang the chorus a few more times to get them seated, then I introduced Jerry and sat down.

Jerry talked a few minutes' and asked me to read the text, he had chosen from the Prophets. He did the best preaching I had ever heard it was great, then he started to call out people to pray over them as usual. That's when my heart began to quiver. The first one he called was Bob.

I prayed "lord this is their first time here" Jerry took Bob's hand and said, "you have been sick, you had a heart problem" Bob said "yes". I turned to someone and said "Jerry is right on" I knew that that was true. Bob had been in Florida a few months earlier and been hospitalized there.

Jerry just kept on and called Georgianna up there. He told her "you have been in the hospital for a while." "Yes" she said, and Jerry prayed for them. It was the best he had ever done, just perfect.

It was a great lose, to the church when Jerry past into the blue a few years ago. A job well done, my Brother.

AMBER DEAD OR ALIVE

A beautiful 21 year, old, girl, that I knew got sick. She was pregnant and that kicked in her sickle cell anemia. I knew her mother, so I knew, she had the disease.

When she got hospitalized Cleve and I started going up to pray for her every week. With my work I lost track of the case and did not know that she had worsened. About three months into the case she went into a coma.

After Christmas, her Grandmother called me with bad news. "They have told us that Amber is going to die tonight." My heart sank. "Can you take me up there? Everybody else is there and I don't have a way"? I said I will be there as soon as I can and hung up the phone. I just literally collapsed on the floor and told God "I am not going to do this funeral. You are going to have to do something".

We got to the hospital about eight thirty. I saw about 23 people there. There were family members in from everywhere. In the group were young girls, her roommates from school. It was pain full just to sit there in that group, waiting for the news, that we were sure would be bad.

I am the man of God to these people and I can't function. Through the pain of this situation I am stunned. I keep praying trying to get a word from the Lord, but nothing happens. Finally, around 10PM. I say, we just can't sit here and let this happen, and I stand up and put my hands out to take the hands next to me. We all stand up and hold hands and begin to pray over this little girl. In part of my prayer I told the Lord, "We can't take her home like this, you have to do something."

We thanked and praised Him and sat down. Then God raised Amber from the dead.

I cannot explain what happened next or why the Doctor acted as he did, but at 2:30 a.m. the Doctor stuck his head around the door and looked troubled. All he said was "I don't know what to tell you, all her vital signs are normal."

Then he shut the door, and we rejoiced in the Lord! She was not dead she was alive! They were prepared to give us a dead young girl before mid-night, but now she was alive.

They kept her in the hospital until she delivered her baby's. She had been pregnant with twins and they were going to die within her, the hospital said that they could not live outside the womb.

Would you like to hear the rest of the story? I just met her for the first time in many years last year. She told me that her children are healthy. Her son has been inducted into the Army and is a paratrooper. She herself has never had a relapse into sickle cell either. She was ecstatic and hugged me for all she was worth. Love never fails.

OUR GOD IS AN AWESOME GOD, AMEN.

CENTRAL AMERICA

We started going to a friend's church and found it a very special experience. To this day it remains one of the highlights of my life.

It was there that I got involved with a group that was going on a 15-20 day mission trip to Central America. I was able to raise the money and off we went. We flew to Florida, changed planes and flew to Managua, Nicaragua C.A. We ministered to people in Guatemala and Nicaragua. The team, built, feeding stations by day and preached in country church's by night. There had been an earthquake and thousands were homeless and destitute of food and clothing.

One of the churches was a small garage by an ally. They would pull the Pulpit and the pews out of the garage and worship in the ally.

In one of the churches the only difference in the height of the platform and the floor was that they had dug the floor one shovel deeper.

In this church when the alter service was given; we were mobbed with people wanting prayer so much so, that we could not move. We could only pray for those that we could touch.

Here was poverty beyond belief; yet here was joy unspeakable. I never met a complainer or whiner; they truly seemed to be happy in the Lord. That trip left a powerful impression on me.

OTHER DREAMS

Twice I have had God give me dreams when I was unemployed. Once I dreamt that a man offered me a job and I agreed to work for him. In the dream, I was driving an old army jeep, and as I drove off, the road got muddy, very muddy. I was afraid I was going to get stuck, but the road turned down hill. I was driving faster because I could see at the bottom the road went up hill again. The mud got to be two feet thick and I was afraid I would get stuck, I just barely made it to the top.

A few weeks later my phone rang, it was a man I had worked for, a few years before. He had been a good man to work for. He paid $10 dollars an hour, and was always on the job, pushing. He said that he had a job building an addition. What will you pay? I asked. What do you want? He replied. You know what I want. OK, he said. I wanted $20 an hour. I hung up the phone amazed.

We started work, the addition was twice as large as the existing house, and there were no plans. Finally, the owner showed me a set that he had. The boss would come each morning and drop off a crew of men and leave. He would get them at closing time look at the progress and leave. No complaints. I needed to dig down 13 feet to make the basement, so he brought in an excavator. I had never run one, so here goes.

I cut the basement into a 45% bank with the front at the bottom of the hill. Try to cut a level floor into a bank the first time you ever used one. The Lord is good.

He told me how deep to go, based on digging for the footer, and then set the footer and poured the concrete. The block layers built the walls and then the cement finishers did the floor. At this point He asked the owner for more money, and the owner balked. He had under bid the job by $60,000 to $75,000 dollars and the owner put him off the property.

He called me later with another job, this was a church. I felt sure that we could do this.

The pastor had brought a property with a metal building to use as a church. The agreement was that within 5 years they would brick it. They were doing better than that. They had poured a footer around the building and extended it another 125 feet down one side. We were going to frame a wall all around the building and then brick it. I laid it all out and they built it, including framing it so we could just slide the existing windows out to the exterior of the walls. Perfect, then we set the trusses and did the roof plywood.

As I stood on the roof one day, I had my second heart Attack. I dropped my tools and caught the ambulance to UHC. I had been off the job 4-6 days, they just need to clean out a stint. When I returned,

I found my boss in a walker, with an incredible story. After I left, He had fallen off the roof and broken his ribs on the air-conditioner, was taken to UHC treated and released.

Now there is only $5,000 dollars left to finish the job, with putting the shingles on and finishing the front portico. More than a month's work and no pay till we are finished. The men walked off the job. There is nothing more I can do, so I pick up my tools and equipment and leave. Well the dream showed a very muddy road, maybe I should have payed attention.

In a final dream I had about employment. I dreamed that a man that resembled my father offered me a job. I had forgotten about the dream and one day coming home from Clarksburg, I stopped at a used furniture store.

When I walked in, there was a man looking at furniture with his back to me. When he turned around, I saw that it was Charlie Thyer, Hi Charlie, how've you been. We talked awhile and then he asked are you working anywhere, at the moment. I answered no, so we talked about me working for him and I agreed.

He had 17 apartments and needed a handy man, right up my ally. Indeed, he was built like my dad and had a very similar make up. We hit it off right away, yet we couldn't have more different. He was Catholic and I'm Pentecostal. You won't believe it, but it was like a hand in a glove, we really enjoyed each other.

At lunch or after work we used to discuss politics and religion all the time and never got mad. He was a Spirit filled, born again, Tongue talking Catholic. I know, I know, you are just going to have to learn that with God all things are possible. God doesn't do everything as I see it either.

Even at Charlies funeral his daughters said, we could never figure out how you and dad got along so well. They said you two got along better then we and dad got along. To God be all the praise.

One of the biggest problems I feel that we as religious people have, is that no one else can be right unless they join our group. How prideful, of course we all want to be right, but we are humans trying to figure out God. Come on give yourself a break. You can't be right. I'm right. OK. (You can laugh)

The reality is that God expects us to love each other because if we have been born again, then we are brothers by birth not theology. Not all the brothers in any family get along or see everything in the same way. Let's give each other some slack and believe that God can bring us into maturity as we grow in grace and in the knowledge of Jesus Christ our Lord.

VICTORY FOR A QUEEN

Once I preached that if you wanted anything more than you wanted God you were in trouble, the next day a deer could run into your car. The daughter of a fine family was driving her new white Cadillac on the way to work, the next day. Then a deer hit her car and came in through the windshield. She was not hurt and when she used the breaks the deer rolled out of the car. She continued to her office and left the car in the parking lot and went into the building. Her boss saw the car and came to see her.

How are you? I can't believe that your, not hysterical! She said the preacher had told her last night in church that it would happen. She just calmly did her work. Later her mother, told me that she had always had this yearning for a white Cadillac, but not anymore, it's gone now.

THE TENT

One day while on my way to work driving through town, I noticed an Evangelist setting a large tent for meetings. He was Ted Shuttlesworth, a very-well known, Evangelist. I saw that there was only four of five men to help him set the tent, so I pulled in. He told me that this was all he had. I went to call my boss to see if I could get the day off. Sure, she said. I helped them all morning till the lunch break.

I was the oldest one there, so I laid down on the grass to rest while the younger men went to the store for lunch meat, but they wouldn't leave me there. Come with us, no I said I'll eat whatever you bring back. They insisted, and again I said no, I am too tired. They insisted again so I got up and went with them.

I just wondered around while they shopped. "Come here" a voice said. "Come here", it was Martha from the church in Dola. She led, me up a side isle and handed me and envelope, which contained $1,000 dollars.

She told me that that morning the Lord told her that she would meet me today and that she should give that money to me. It was the tithes on a government check that they got after I had prayed for them.

There is no way I would have been in that store or met her that day except by the will of God. See for yourself, count the steps that lead to this meeting. Friend when God wants to do something in your life, no power on earth can stop Him.

THE MISSION

I don't remember the year, but for a whole year I was asked to teach on Thursday nights, in the Mission. Now teaching to addicts in a mission is a rare experience. At first, I just did what I supposed everyone did, I taught on salvation. I just started to teach that we are all sinners and in need of a savior. That God had sent His Son Jesus to die for our sins. That if we would believe on Him, we could be saved from our sins.

So, for several weeks I kept on this line, until I felt the Spirit said. "Teach on tithing". I said they don't have any money. He said. "Teach on tithing". And so, I argued with God for three weeks. Have you won any of those, me neither? I felt stupid, but I started teaching on tithing at the mission. I didn't get the point but week by week I "taught on tithing".

There was, and there always will be someone that makes a fuss, a woman there at the end of every teaching would say. Jesus said, "The poor you will have with you always." I acknowledged the verse, but I had no rebuttal.

Next week it was the same thing. I gave the lesson and she made the same quote. I still couldn't think up an answer. I dreaded the third week, but I went, still no answer.

At the close of the lesson, she stood up again and said, "The poor you will have with you always." Now, I felt the Spirit stir within me and I said "Yes, but He doesn't want you to be one of them". What a powerful affirmation of the love of God. That even to these who had nothing, those that were the cast offs of the earth. He wanted them to arise and take hold of His promises and find the life He offered them. What a Mighty God we serve. Love beyond description, Mercy without measure.

Can I tell you the rest of the story? One man came to me a few weeks later and said I've got a job delivering papers. One of them told me, I don't live here any- more. I got me a room at the Johnson Hotel. Now you and I wouldn't want to have to live there, but it is one step above living in the mission.

God saw what you and I could never see. His love and His power, defies, the logic of men and the power of Satan.

A Baptist lay-preacher built a motel and at least two women at the mission got jobs as maids there. One day a woman called me and asked if I would help her pick out a car she said, I don't know how to pick out a good one".

If you want me to explain to you how this all happened, how they got the money." Go talk to my Father, all I can tell you is that "He made it happen." Sooner or later we are going to learn that He does the impossible every day, because that is who He is. "He is able to do exceedingly abundantly above all that we could ever ask or think," every day. Eph 3:20.

PASTOR T.D. JONES

Whenever I read scriptures about humility, I think of Pastor Jones. I know hundreds of ministers around the World, but you would be hard pressed to find a more, humble man than he.

He is the only man that I have been around a lot that is willing to work with any group or on any project without it being his idea, or him having to run it. Time after time I saw him give the credit to someone else for an idea that he came up with.

In all the years in the church that he Pastored, I watched him stand in the shadows and lavish praise on others. He stood firm for what he believed and was unyielding in his lifestyle, but compassionate in his dealings with his fellow man.

Of all the ministers I know he was the most tender with those who seemed to stumble more than the rest. His goal was to lift-up the fallen, not to condemn them.

One time when I was working on his house, he was going to hug me, and I said I'm dirty. His answer "your, not dirty". In times when I have tried and failed some test and asked Jesus to forgive me, I have thought of those words "Your, not dirty". I would be glad to stand as strong and be as humble as T. D. Jones.

The thing that in all my life has amazed me most about God, is that when he wants you to do something for him nothing or no one, can stand in your way.

One time I told Nathan that I was tired and did not think that I would go back into ministry anymore. I was going on 70 and felt wore out.

One Sunday as I was leaving church, I had one foot out the door and I heard someone say they are looking for a Pastor over there. Where I asked? In Jordan. They just got a new Pastor a year ago. Yes, they said, but they just let him go.

I thought about that as I drove home. I tried to find the number but could not. I looked in the paper for the ad, it was not there. Nathan knew, but because I said, "I am tired", he did not tell me. Finally, after a few weeks I found the number.

In a few days we made contact. He told me that there were some ministers already signed up. I said that's alright, put my name in if you want to, or not as you feel led, he signed me up. I was scheduled to preach in about 12 weeks.

At a convention at Pastor John's 6 weeks later a prophet from Maryland felt he had a "Word from the Lord" for me. "My son, don't be troubled rest in me I shall bring it to pass." Then 3 weeks later he phoned me and said. They are going to offer you the church, take it. They don't have much money to pay you, take what, they offer.

The Thursday after that my phone rings. "George the preacher we had scheduled for Sunday called, to cancel can you preach"? Yes, I answered. I preach and go home. My regular day comes, I preach again and go home. This time I pack all my church library and put it in the car.

They are supposed to decide that Wednesday, but I don't get a call. The next week I call. Who did you pick? "No one, we are having some that we liked, preach again. You are to preach again". So, I preach again, still no call.

Wednesday a few weeks later as church is in the closing prayer my phone rings and I run outside to open it. "You are our new Pastor, can you come over tonight to share your vision"? Yes, and we drive over.

THE CHURCH

I shared my vision and answered their questions. Then they asked how much money I wanted. I pretended I did not hear and talked with some of them. Then he said that all they could afford, was a few hundred dollars per week, I told them that that was fine.

We started at the new church. God immediately began to show approval of me as His choice. He already had saved them from one situation and soon another one sprouted up.

In less than two months two members got into a squabble and in a meeting they both brought letters of resignations. I gave one of them time off from his duties to rest, and I told the other that I would not accept that letter of resignation. So, both families stayed, and the steam was released.

One of the board members cried, he said I thought that this was the end of the church. They were all relieved. For a year and a half, it looked as if this was going to be good.

Several new people came and stayed. An old preacher and his wife came, and everyone loved them. We still see them from time to time. We Had sings and dinners and even some improvements to the property. We saw God touch lives, and a few saints went to be with the Lord.

The building was two buildings butted to each other, with no interior connecting stairway. You had to go outside to the church offices, and the classrooms. The kitchen and dining room were under the classrooms and there was a way to the sanctuary from there, but not from the classrooms themselves.

One day I thought that the back of the rear bedroom would be in line with the wall of the steps if we should build, an interior set of steps. I asked if they would like to have the two buildings connected by interior steps. The elders said, "Yes".

I tested the idea by drilling a small hole from the rear closet wall from the hallway into the sanctuary, it came out exactly where we all wanted it to. They said go ahead and in a few, months-time, we had a useable access to the church offices and the Sunday school rooms. An added, bonus was two more bathrooms for all to use, now a total of six. Every-one was really, happy with the new addition to the church.

A big problem was that we didn't seem to gain any new members after the first two years. At the same time, I asked the worship team women to ware, skirts or dresses when they were going to be on the platform. Most of them agreed

The worship leader was a young woman and kept nice scarves on the platform for any woman, who's blouse was too revealing. She was a great worship leader and a great help to me, in these areas. She and her husband were great assets to our church.

THE CAMP MEETINGS

Sandy and I had already been invited to fellowship with a new group. They were into camp meetings. On our first meeting with them at Sister Sisler's church in a nearby city; they invited Sandy and I to work the altars with their people.

One thing I liked about this group was that they spent a lot of time praying with people at the altar. Some-times they would stay nearly an hour. They would stay, as long, as there was a need, and we liked that.

While we prayed one evening, I noticed a woman really lost in worship at the altar. She was worshiping in tongues and in English, she was trembling, and the tears flowed freely.

As I was moved by her worship the Spirit said to me "She is really hurting." I turned to look again and said, "It doesn't look like it to me, and He said it a second time "She is really hurting."

When she relaxed, I started. Sister, I know that you don't know me, but as you worshiped, I believed the Spirit said. That you are in great pain. "I am", she cried and took me to the front pew.

Our youngest child was killed." I was stunned. She continued; "I have not been able to forgive him or speak peaceably to him ever since. I go to church and pray and ask God to help me, but when I get face to face with him, I lose it and get angry with him." Then she told me the rest of the story.

She told me that they had had a wonderful marriage, that they were in a really good church, they were all happy, and got along great.

Then an accident had taken the life of their daughter. I could not figure out how they were still alive. Only the Grace of God could have gotten them this far.

So, for the last five years they had been in this pain, trying to hold on to their sanity, their marriage, and themselves. This moment could change everything. I told her that God would not have shown me this, unless He was planning to fix it.

We prayed that God would heal their hearts, and she went home. The family and their church was happy with what God was doing for them. I am always ecstatic when the Lord steps into a situation like this.

About six months later at another meeting, she introduced me to her husband. She told me that they were going on a honeymoon, their first vacation in years. I was so glad to see them I just loved on them, and after the meeting they went home. The Lord is so good. Praise His name. It was just nice to know that God wanted to save their marriage.

MEAN WHILE BACK AT WORK

Still working for the landlord, a woman with 5 girls, had a ground floor apartment. One day Charlie rented the upstairs apartment to a single older man. The man bothered me. At first, I just didn't like the way he talked about Charlie, but there was something else. I just felt uneasy about him in my spirit. I didn't know why. As I was working around the property one day, I saw him talking with the woman and really felt nervous about that, because she had 5 little girls. I told her to be careful about him, I didn't know why. A little while later Charlie put him out. The woman showed me on her smart phone, that he was a registered sex offender.

He had conned Charlie into getting the apartment without filling out the paper work, that's why Charlie had put him out. It was marvelous how God had spared that woman and her children from all that pain. He would have molested them for sure.

AN ASSISTANT

Sandy and I fellowship, a number, of church's and in one of them I felt to prophecy over a young brother. He was helping the Pastor and seemed very faithful. I asked the Pastor to come with me, as we were in his church. The man's name was Dick. I prophesied that he was to be the assistant Pastor to the minister. The pastor, told me that was what he had seen in the man. I was being used as conformation. God is good.

CAMP MEETINGS

At the camp meetings, we stayed from three – five days on the grounds. Usually there were three meetings a day with three meals being served. The best camp ground that we have been to so far was at Fairchance. At Fairchance there were cabins, dorms and camper spots. They have an awesome old Tabernacle and new dining hall.

Camp meetings are so exciting. There is a great anointing, great worship and great preaching. Healings and miracles take place, and there is great fellowship and food. What's not to like, they really build up the saints, and minister to the needy.

About 10 years ago I began to ask the Lord if we could have a camper to go to the camp meetings with. At one of the local conventions we met a man that had a real nice 35' motor home, but he wanted $10,000 dollars for it, a really good price. We only had $ 0 dollars to buy one. The next year he said that he would sell it to us for $5,000 dollars. So, we put "for sale" signs on some property my wife owned in the woods. Just bare wooded lots, but two of them sold within 24 hours.

The others have never sold. Now we had our motor home and it was a beauty. We have gone to camp meetings for the last nine years in it. Praise be to the Lord.

Over the years we have been to camp meetings in Ohio, Pa and West Virginia, and have never been disappointed. One of the joys is meeting people that you see only once a year at that camp meeting. We have friends from all over the country that we have met at the camp meetings. Many of them we keep in touch with by phone. We have always seen healings and miracles at the camp meetings.

THE NEW CAMP MEETINGS

The biggest organization was in Pennsylvania. A few years ago; the overseer notified us all that he was giving them up due to poor health He mentioned that he was turning the organization over to Bishop Yoder of Maryland, as temporary overseer till they could vote in who they wanted. At the meeting to vote to elect new officers, we elected for Bishop Yoder to stay as the overseer, for two years, I believe.

At the next camp meeting we confirmed Bishop Yoder and the other officers for their term. At another camp meeting they surprised me by making me a Bishop under Bishop Yoder.

We are still having our own camp meetings but love to fellowship others also. We are small, but, growing and are trying to be led of the Spirit. We work as a team, no one pushing his or her agenda, just blending together as a body in Christ.

In some of the camp meetings, I have prophesied to some people. About events in their life. To one woman I felt that she was having emotional problems because she had been locked in a dark closet, when she was a child, by her parents when she was bad. Her husband confirmed that that was true.

A second time while a woman was praying at the altar, I felt to pray for her and told her that she needed to let go of the past. That the past was keeping her from moving into her future, she denied that. Later at snack time she came to me and said, you have gotten closer to me than anyone else did. Thank the Lord.

A close minister friend of mine had to retire because of sickness in his family. They asked me to preach there one Sunday. I believed the Lord gave me a message for them. That they should find a younger preacher, one in his fifties, which they did. While there I felt the Lord telling me that a young man in the back of the sanctuary had a calling to the ministry. The Pastor confirmed that to me later.

VISITATION III

This would be the third time that God would visit me personally. I had been sick with the flu for 4 or 5 weeks and was not getting any better. Saturday night as I turned to go upstairs to bed Sandy asked, "Are we going to church tomorrow"? My answer was "it doesn't look like it now".

I felt, miserable, sleep came fitfully, but eventually I drift off. At 5AM I have a dream or visitation. Jesus walks into my room and up to my side. He lays His hand on my shoulder and says, "You are healed", and I was. I sat up on the side of the bed and was totally healed. He was gone. We got up, ate breakfast and got ready for church. Praise be to the Lord.

AND THEN THERE WAS WATSON

Who could forget, Watson? The family had been old World aristocrats. They had moved here years ago from the South and started a business. I had never met his father, but his mother was a wonderful lady, the last of a vanishing class. Watson and his twin brother were the last of the line.

Watson had been the, store to store salesman and as such he had a car. His brother was not able to do much and died in his 40's I believe. They were Methodist and normally Watson went to his mothers, church after she passed on; but he did have a circuit. For several months he might go to a church in the Valley. Then to his mother's church. When he found out that we had opened the Tabernacle, he would visit with us for several months, before moving on.

Watson was different, he didn't think as others, he was a free thinker. As such you never knew what he would do.

One of the favorite things he often did was to preach with me. When I said something that stirred him, he would jump to his feet and begin preaching to add to what I was saying. I loved it, it excited the people, and we all laughed and went along with him. He kept the meeting rolling. But poor Cleve got confused and would ask Watson to sit down, while he was preaching.

I learned only later that Watson had died in another church during the service years before I met him. He had had a heart attack and been pronounced dead by a Registered nurse. As he laid there on the sanctuary floor the Pastor prayed the prayer of faith over Watson and God raised him from the dead. Everybody loved Watson.

When they opened the casket for the final viewing and I got to see Watson for the last time, I thought about that verse of the song. "I wasn't there when they nailed Him to the tree, I wasn't there when they laid Him in the tomb, but I'll be there when they offer Him the Crown". See, you latter my brother.

SO HOW DOES IT ALL END

Do you think that most of the people's lives end up like mine? What about the mentally challenged or street people? What percentage of people, whose lives start with the pain of parental abuse get the help they need?

You can all see that my life was nothing less than miraculous. I know that I would have become a killer, there is not the slightest doubt of that. Someday, a Police Officer would have had to shoot me down, or I would have had to spend, my last days in a federal prison, but there is another group of people out there.

THE PAIN

Here's a case in point. Could they be more common than we realize?

She seemed normal. She had a husband that seemed normal at first glance. They had 4 children that were anything but normal. Her husband had lost his job in another State, and they had to move back to her family's home.

Her husband was tense, and I thought it was that he had lost his job and needed to find employment. I thought that when he was back to work, he would calm down. Men don't like being out of work they feel that they are not doing their part of taking care of their family or fulfilling their obligations.

He worked fine helping me do the work that his mother had hired me to do, but I began, to notice, that he yelled at his wife and kids. Once his wife was leaving with the three youngest children and as she left the house he comes running after her yelling "Where exactly are you going"? I thought how exactly does it matter? She's got the kids, she's not leaving you. His oldest daughter was sitting next to me on the front porch swing crying. He yelled for her, "get in here and do the dishes." I told her that this is not her fault, that there is something wrong in his head. She got up and did the dishes.

As time would pass, I would pick up the story piece by piece. He had always been like this. He had abused his wife and yelled at her almost from the beginning. He had screamed at all of them all their lives.

She had wanted to take the children and run back to her home, but that would have meant crossing State lines. He had warned her that if she ran, he would have had her arrested for kidnapping.

When he lost his job, they had no place to go but to her home here. His mother was snippy with me, she wanted me to hurry. She said this was costing her too much money. I could see in her, his problem. She had abused him, perhaps even her husband, who knows.

She; was definitely, a tyrant, a controlling woman. But who had abused her, on and on it goes and where it stops, nobody knows. In prison, on drugs, alcohol in a hospital or in the casket.

In this case he left her for another woman that he could more easily control. The reason that he left her was that she had ended up on crutches. Where do you go when you are trapped in a violent, relationship?

Unfortunately, most of the time into the back of your head, that's right. You build a hiding place in your sub-conscious mind. Little by little she gave up the fight, and in her mind, she collapsed, then she fell in the shower.

She needed a cane and a walker, but that didn't bring any sympathy. He continued to yell at her, and she needed more relief. She finally divorced him; then he left, he had found another woman, he didn't need her anymore.

She remarried 5 years latter to a man that had three young children and the pressure of having this violent past and now 7 children with not much help from her new husband pushed her into a wheelchair. She divorced her second husband and is out of the wheelchair and doing much better.

She and her children were still in emotional hiding. It seemed to them that they all had a strange affliction. The oldest, a girl, seemed silent, a non-verbal person. She slept most of the time, she was in depression. The, oldest boy, is full of hate. He hates his father. He is angry with his mother for not protecting them; He is full of rage, but she was under fire all the time too.

The next is a girl that just laid in bed all the time, with what I believe a sickness caused by having to live with abuse. The middle boy just sits and plays on the lap top all the time he is awake. He acts like a comedian when he does talk. The little boy is much less hurting, He cooks and cleans and uses the laptop, and he will talk with me and show me how to do things. Thank God as time passes they are getting better.

The help that they have gotten, for the children is that they all have been in the boy scouts since they were old enough. The second blessing is that they were in good church's and home schooled through high school. The two youngest are still being home schooled.

The home school organization they are with does a lot of group activities, including meeting every Monday at a church for a day of making things with their hands. They go on school trips for historic class work. Being with others has helped them all. They have also been into some counselling.

Multiply this case a million times and you can begin to feel the pain. We need to stop the abuse of parents upon their children, now.

REVELATION

Revelation, sometimes comes in strange packages. I have always known that even being a Christian, that even walking in the Spirit, there were many times I did not give in to the Spirit. There has always been this, of me first. I have always been fascinated with guns. Now understand me I am through with hate, I do not want to kill anyone anymore, but from a child I wanted to be a soldier.

Just after we got married, I got drafted. When I got to the induction center the female Lieutenant, said "If there is any reason that you shouldn't be here, it is too late now." I showed her a Doctors slip that said my wife was pregnant. She said that by law they couldn't take me, so she dismissed me, and I went home, more honeymoon. But I have always wanted to be a soldier.

Sometimes I wanted a gun so bad that I spent money for the gun that I should have spent on the family or to pay bills. Sometimes it was a car. Sometimes it was a tool. I hope not always, but I know that many times I put myself ahead of the needs or interests of my wife and family. They always had the bare necessities, but they could have had more if I not been so selfish. I learned selfishness because of hate.

THE CONNECTION

I had prayed many times to the Lord for help in overcoming my selfishness, and I have improved over the years, and then it happened. In and about the year 2000, in the studying of the lives of serial killers, I saw myself.

They were like me, I would have ended up like them if Jesus hadn't come into my life as he did. He saved me, he gave me eternal life, but I was required to grow up in Him. I had majored in miners. I had mastered to an extent, the 5 things Jesus sent us to do. Preach the gospel, heal the sick, raise the dead, cast out demons and cleans the lepers. What I had not done, was to crucify the flesh. Sometimes, I would work on myself when I was embarrassed by my lack of Christ likeness.

In following a story that was unfolding in the newspapers and on T.V. they finally captured a man that had been killing women, for about 10 years.

As the story unfolded, I began to see myself in him and saw a pattern in the lives of these types of men.

The way they were raised by their mothers had some similarities to the way my mother raised me. Their mothers were very troubled, they had a very difficult and controlling relationship with their husbands, just as mom had with dad.

These men's mothers were very high strung, so was mom, she seemed to tremble, as if she was chewing when she was angry. Their mothers were very harsh with their husbands, so was mom, with my dad. Their mothers broke plates over their husband's head, mom through plates and hot coffee at dad. Their father would just walk away, so did my dad.

In this violent atmosphere, they learned to fear and hate their mother, I learned to hate mine. Some of them were bed wetter's, so was I. The stress of being raised in a violent home is the reason for this.

It caused them to desire to gain control over women, which was a very similar feeling that was in my heart. I was not going to let any woman do to me as my mother had done to my dad.

Their mothers had trained them to kill by filling them with hate for her, just as my mother had done. It was clear for me to see that some of their thoughts were almost the same as mine. They thought of killing her and burning the house down around her, that had been very similar to the hate driven thoughts that had been in my head, as a 19, year old boy. My mother was training me to hate women and to kill them.

As a child you can't hate your parents, you want to love them, but you don't have to love strangers, you can kill them. You believe that all women are just like your mother, and all men are just like your father.

What happens is that in your sub-conscious mind, you can't separate women from your mother. If you hate your mother then you hate all women, if you hate your father then you hate all men, sub-consciously.

What happened to me was that I met Jesus Christ and He saved me. I got cleansed from the power of the hate that my mother instilled in me, but I have never been completely able to trust woman.

These serial killers, never met Jesus Christ and as a, result they went on to kill many women, to get back at their mothers for the abusing their fathers and humiliating them.

We just keep passing the abuse on and on. If I had not met Jesus, I would have kept passing the pain on to my children and they would pass it on and on and on.

JESUS, THE HEALING OF HIS LOVE

Here we see the awesome truth "ALL BEHAVIORS ARE LEARNED BEHAVIORS". We are what we have heard and seen, mostly from our parents. The amazing reality is that if children are shown unconditional love by their parents, they will not easily be taken down the darksome path of destruction.

It is mostly the children of abusive parents that get into smoking, drugs, alcohol, and sex; because they need something to fill the void of not being loved. When a child does not feel loved by his/her parents that leaves an emptiness that must be filled. For a child to be whole they need to feel the love of their parents and the love of God.

MY 60 YEARS

I have been in Christian ministry to people for at least 60 years. Ministry to people is not just preaching. The real work is to help those who are troubled with life's pain. Terrible things have happened to them and their lives are in shambles. Take divorce, for instance. There are no winners in any divorce. Both the adults suffer, but the real losers are the children.

In one case recorded in the "Readers Digest"1 A couple divorce's and have one son. The mother tries for several years to take the boy from his father, but the court finds insufficient evidence. Finally, she fakes a rape. The husband spends 81 days in jail, but the court finds him innocent. The proof is beyond question; but the judge still gives them equal visitation. The, adults pass their pain onto their children. The children, of divorce, are most often very troubled youth. 1 Readers Digest, Dec. /Jan. 2011,/12. Pg. 188. "Caught in a trap". 33 out of every 100 men accused of rape were framed. "Police files" before DNA.

I told my son's when they were dating "be careful how you break up with a girl. And don't start dating another girl for several months, or the first girl might charge you with rape for breaking up with her. That is a very common emotion in women; and a very common way of their dealing with being dropped.

I have noticed that all the cases of bipolar disorder that I have dealt with had at least one parent that got in their child's face and screamed at them most of the time. All but two of the Prostitutes I have talked with, were molested by their father. The others, one had her mother start her in the business; the other, her brother held her down while his friend raped her.

In the case of transgender. A woman wanted a little girl after having sons, but the next child was a boy. He had baby blue eyes and curly blond hair; he was so cute. In private she dressed him in panties, and nighties. She called him sweetie, baby doll, honey and told him how pretty he was. This goes on for 8 or 9 years, so when he is a teenager who is he/she?

Mothers that abuse their husbands can produce boys that become serial killers. Fathers that abuse their wives can produce daughters that kill. They usually get work in hospitals and they sometimes kill male patience. Mostly they just kill their lovers, like the black widow killer and the waitress in Texas.

Fathers that terrorize their daughters can produce Lesbians. Most are too afraid to be intimate with men, so it is easy for them to form relationships with other women. The same is true with men that as boys were terrified by their mothers. Many live, in fear that they will not be accepted by straights, so sometimes they commit suicide after a few years.

Some, as one woman wrote in a "Dear Abby" newspaper column, said that she didn't feel being a lesbian was a choice. Then she tells her story. She said that her father had molested her. That her first husband had abused her, that her second husband had abused her. Then she fell into the arms of a woman. You would have too, if you had been through all that.

Some, as one girl wrote, get taken by surprise. She came from a small town and had won a scholarship to a large college in the mid-west. She was put into a girl's dorm with another girl athlete. That girl was a lesbian. She seemed very friendly; little by little she started touching her. First a foot rub then a back rub, then finally a night in bed. When she woke up, she said at least I won't get pregnant; which her mother was worried about.

At the club they told her that she was born a homosexual and not to worry about it. She began to notice that one by one the homosexuals were committing suicide. She finally went home and told her parents and her church and started getting help. Today she is strong and growing up in the Lord as a young lady, and is moving on. Book by Mary Whelchel "If you only knew" Pgs. 60-70.

Each case is different, but 90% of maladjusted teens and young adults, are the results of bad, and or abusive parenting. Most people that are out of the range we call normal are that way because they were abused. You can put a label on it. You can proscribe a pill for it, but we can stop it by sharing the love of Jesus Christ.

LGBTQ-XYZ "ALL BEHAVIOR IS LEARNED BEHAVIOR"

Legalizing, bad behavior will not help those who are disturbed by what has happened to them. They need our help and our unconditional love.

If you are one who is fraught with fears or worry about life, about why you feel out of sort with life, or family or the world in general, please get help. Don't just sit there with pain that you can't resolve. There are people that want to help you.

If you had a broken bone, we would rush you to a hospital to get help. Please don't be embarrassed by emotional brokenness. There is help. You probably prayed to God for help when you felt the need, but you didn't seem to get it. That doesn't mean that He doesn't care. He cares, he cared so much that he sent his son to die for you. He will help you to move on if you'll invite him into your life now.

EPILOGUE

As I wind down this writing, I want you to know that you are just the same as I am. I was a product of my upbringing, the same as you. There were people that were trying to help me, you can find them.

My dad took abuse to help me the only way he knew. The resident State Trooper tried his best. A Pastor risked everything to help me, but I needed to let them.

We all need the help of other people, we need to take their Godly advice, and their help. We are the offspring of God, only He can fill that void inside us. Only in Christ Jesus can we be made whole.

When children are trapped in abusive situations for any length of time, they become abnormal. Please be one of the hero's that sees these children and loves them back to health. Stop the carnage, report child abuse, now, today.

As I look back over my 80 years, I keep asking why did He pick me? In this book we see only the highlights, of the working of God in my life. My life has been the most awesome life that I could have dreamed of.

My marriage with Sandy has made me a better human being. She truly has been my helpmate. Our children have taught me many things, about growing up in God. Our grand-children are a real blessing to us, Caleb made my learning to use this "lap top" possible.

There were many people down through the years that put into my life the God concept. The reality that Jesus Christ is real, and that the Bible is the truth. That Gods way is the only way that works.

You can prove it for yourself. Just ask Him to forgive you of your sins and to come into your life and be your Lord. Jesus died upon the cross and shed His blood to cleanse us from our sins and free us from our past. Especially, if you were the abused, and you were the one that was devastated, you will be set free from the pain full results of a broken life.

In your mind you are wasted, you can never get it right, you have failed, but that's not true. Let Jesus into your heart and He will rebuild your life just as He did mine. He waits for you, He longs to hold you in His arms, and start to restore all that the Devil, and people have taken from you.

Start right now. There is a good church near you. They will not judge you they will help you. Ask "Jesus to come into your heart and forgive you of your sins. Say "I want to be yours forever, thank you in Jesus name, Amen". Then you can wash away your sins in the waters of baptism and pray to be baptized with the Holy Spirit for the power to live above sin and serve God every day, you can do it.

Just as sure as I have written this there will be some out there that will say "he made at least some of this stuff up." That is the proof of what I have been saying about myself all along. He saw in me what I would have never seen in myself. He saw what He could do with one solitary life that could be surrendered to Him.

It is not about us, you or me. What you do with your life is what you let Jesus do with it. You can surrender to the pain, you can say my parents did me in; they destroyed me and there is nothing I can do, to change. But that's not true.

You can give into hate and let the Devil destroy you. You can get rich and powerful through giving into hate; but it will also bring you down. Many a Doctor, lawyer, or famous person, became powerful on the hate that drove them; only to end up on skid-row, or in prison. You don't want to go there.

Please let go of the anger, the hate, and the unforgiveness; and throw yourself on the mercy of God. They were wrong, they abused you, and they molested you; but leave their punishment with God. You can be set free from the pain that they inflicted upon you by turning them over to God and letting go of the hate or bitterness in your heart. Forgive them; it will set you free; that's right, it will set you free.

In their evil unless they repent, they will end up in hell; you don't want to be there with them. Let them go and give it all to Jesus; ask his forgiveness for your sins and ask him to be your Lord and savior.

He will walk with you and give you the victory over your past life. He has promised you an abundant life, a life more awesome than you can possibly understand, He really has. John 10:10. Says I am come that you might have life and have it more abundantly.

How about it, want to try it, it will knock your socks off.!!

I would have never dreamed of a life like mine.

You can have one too. Just believe.

With God's Blessing. Brother, George Freeman

P. S. Last week a woman that is on oxygen, called sandy and I. "Please come and pray for me, I am having trouble breathing. As we prayed over her the most powerful anointing of the Holy Spirit came down upon us and she was heald. Two days later she called almost yelling into the phone and said 'I can breathe better." This week she called to tell us that she was going out that day, the first time in many months. Today now three weeks later she went out again. Praise be to the Lord.

Surrender to Jesus He can make it happen for you. G.B.F.

ABOUT THE AUTHOR

Rev. Freeman has written a very detailed and unequivocal book on his life as a young boy, living under the influence of the anger and abuse heaped upon his father and himself by his mother; which led him into a life of rebellion and violence. Then he reveals how Jesus came to him and caused a three hundred and sixty degree turn around in his life; which caused him to put down the gun and take up the Bible. He describes in detail how his faith in god made him the person he is today. A husband of 57 years; father of two fine sons; four wonderful grand-children and a respected minister of the gospel.

I highly recommend "Bad to the Bone" as a testimony of how you can get beyond the pain of the abuse from your past. Dr. Freeman serves as chairman of our Board of Directors of CMU Theological University.

Dr. Sharon Finney, Th.D. Academic Dean of CMU Theological University

Other book by Author: YOU ARE MADE IN THE IMAGE OF GOD (temporarily out of print)

CPSIA information can be obtained
at www.ICGtesting.com
Printed in the USA
LVHW042201281019
635548LV00002B/341